The Cambridge School of the History of Political Philosophy

Dave McFaul

i

The Cambridge School of the History of Political Philosophy

© 2020 Dave McFaul

Amazon - Kindle Direct Publishing

ISBN: 9798552900169

In loving memory of my mom Anne who was always appreciative and thankful. She loved singing in the choir, babies/children, and Dilly Bars. God smiled upon her and was merciful.

Christian perfection is loving God with all our heart, mind, soul, and strength. This implies that no passions contrary to love remain in the soul. It means that all thoughts, words, and actions are governed by pure love.

John Wesley

Contents

Abstract

The Cambridge School of J. G. A. Pocock and Quentin Skinner is one of the major influences on the philosophy of intellectual history. They've used the post-positivist philosophy of paradigms and speech-acts to illustrate their historical practice. They both studied Machiavelli, Pocock for his ideological paradigm of a new prince using his *virtu* to combat *fortuna* which crowded out those of traditional custom and religious providence, while Skinner studied what Machiavelli did within the tradition of rhetoric, which was to create stricter standards of rationality for political strategies in using historical examples to disprove traditional "moral" speculation. These moves initiated modern political thought.

There is a debate today between positive and negative liberty. Skinner shows Machiavelli believed in negative not positive liberty. Even though he had a theory of human nature that demanded a republic with plenty of offices open to all citizens best served by the virtues, and the law can force us to maintain our freedom such as a citizen's army. Philip Pettit argues there is a difference between interference and domination. The latter is arbitrary, the other can serve our interests according to our understandings and standards. What is needed is democratic avenues to contest government decisions so we can continuously improve our institutions.

Preface

In the fifties Lipsett complained there hadn't been any political philosophy for sixty years. He said it was the fault of positivism which held only those facts verified through the senses, or else tautologies, were true. This made ethics and politics appear to be either arbitrary opinions or lies and nonsense. It also held the human sciences should be modeled after the physical ones; democracy was simply the bargaining between conflicting interests and the public formed no higher unity. In the end positivism was undermined by Thomas Kuhn and John Austin among others. In 1962 Kuhn showed paradigm shifts can change the interpretation of everything, science is not just an accumulation of details. Also in 1962 Austin showed language did more things than just state truth claims.

The Cambridge School of J. G. A. Pocock and Quentin Skinner uses philosophy to illustrate historical points. Skinner uses Austin's speech act theory to describe what an historical agent was doing in the context of their time, the rhetorical tradition says what is to count as a move in a speech act. He attacks a metaphysics of coherence by saying there are no perennial questions and we should not expect to find a systematic philosophy in an author which they never achieved. Pocock has also used Kuhn' theory of paradigms and some terms from structuralism to explain his historical practice. His attack on the metaphysics of coherence is that there are many polyvalent languages in politics that convey several different meanings on numerous levels. For both, once we are aware of the traditions of political languages we can see what innovations an author was actually doing. This takes becoming familiar with a vast number of primary materials in the tradition.

I look at both their studies of Machiavelli and show how Pocock saw the paradigm of a new prince using *virtu* to combat *fortuna* was crowding out custom and religion to begin modern political thought. Skinner looked at the

four-hundred-year tradition of rhetoric that formed
Machiavelli's background. He showed that Machiavelli
imitated a sub-tradition of the genre, advice for princes,
even while he demolished the virtue ethics tradition to
establish his own strategies that followed strict lines of
political reasoning adhering to their own code of
standards: raison d'état.

Finally, two of Skinner's essays on Machiavelli show
the republican did not believe in the positive liberty of
Rousseau's self-rule but the negative liberty of a lack of
restraint. Even still, he had a theory of human nature that
demanded a particular form of polity, with offices open to
all citizens and to be served by the civic virtues. He also
thought good laws could make the anti-social respect and
maintain freedom. Philip Pettit contrasted negative liberty
with non-domination instead. The laws could interfere
with our freedom but that does not necessarily undermine
our liberty, especially if it makes sure others cannot
arbitrarily interfere with us. If government policies serve

the interests of constituents according to their understanding, they don't have to be arbitrary. The only way to ensure this, according to Pettit, is to have avenues available for contesting public decisions. John Maynor adds that not only should we guard against arbitrary domination against ourselves, but we should make sure that we as citizens do not dominate others in turn. This takes civic education.

1: The Dearth of Political Philosophy

Peter Laslett and the Death of Political Philosophy

One of the sources of inspiration for the republican revival was a challenge issued by Peter Laslett who said in his 'introduction' to the first series of *Philosophy, Politics and Society* 'for the moment, anyway, political philosophy is dead.' (1956 p.vii) At least since the idealist Bernard Bosanquet's *The Philosophical Theory of the State* (1890). Some would say the Marxists replaced philosophical analysis with sociology, and this led to the death of political Philosophy. The idea is that Marxists dismiss political philosophy as sociologically determined. Laslett disagreed. A traditional political philosophy could be erected on the Marxist sociology, and the debates between Marxists and their critics observe the conventions of traditional political philosophy. Laslett put the blame squarely on the shoulders of the linguistic

Cambridge School

philosophers: Bertrand Russell, the early Ludwig Wittgenstein, A. J. Ayer, and Gilbert Ryle.

> The Logical Positivists did it. ... [They] called into question the logical status of all ethical statements, setup rigorous criteria of intelligibility which at one time threatened to reduce the traditional ethical systems to assemblages of nonsense. Since political philosophy is, or was, an extension of ethics, the question has been raised whether political philosophy is possible at all. (Laslett 1956, p. lx)

If the only metaphysics bequeathed to us from linguistic analysis involves a metaethics with either an antirealist assumption, that ethical statements are neither true nor false, or Mackie's 'error theory,' where all ethics are lies designed to control the masses, there would then be nothing of substance to political debates. There would be nothing real and concrete that would deserve proper adjudication for either side. The reason Laslett blamed logical positivism so much for the sterility of political philosophy was that it made the discussion of such things appear to be arbitrary opinion rather than rational argument. What really killed political philosophy was the separation of fact and value, along with the belief we lived in a neutral universe.

The Roots of Positivism in the Early American Histories of Political Philosophy

Laslett put the blame for the death of political philosophy squarely on the linguistic philosophers, but American political science has its own home-grown positivism linked to a liberal pluralism. John Gunnell (2013) offers an account of the history of behaviouralism as a political science. There has been some controversy whether the tradition of political philosophy can coexist with political science, a particularly American invention. Behaviouralism was a movement of positivism in the fifties that believed in the unity of science and thought political science should follow the methods of the natural, or "exact," sciences. The foundations for the scientism of

American political science, however, was partially laid by the histories of political philosophy that came before it in the early twentieth century: John Dunning (1902, 1905, 1920) and George Sabine (1939) who opposed the idealist Francis Leiber (1838,1853). Then in the nineteen fifties Behaviouralism took hold as a positivist political social science.

Leiber edited the *Encyclopedia Americana*, and was the father of the American cannon of great political philosophers. He wrote the *Manual of Political Ethics* (1838) and *On Civil Liberty and Self-Government* (1853). He was influenced by German Idealism and the German Historical School. His vision of the State was of a unified society that gave theoretical substance to the idea of popular sovereignty. The community was a majority that preceded government and the constitution. It was to form a coherent whole greater than the sum of its parts. This was replaced by 'pluralism,' the basis for the American political science's version of democracy.

Positivism in political science goes as far back as the beginning. In 1903 political scientists separated themselves from the profession of History to found the American Political Science Association. At the time, John Dunning, Leiber Professor of History and Political Philosophy in the School of Political Science at Columbia University, wrote three volumes of *A History of Political Theories* (1902, 1905, 1920). Dunning was sympathetic to the early positivists Comte and Spencer. He believed in the progress of ideas insofar as false ideas would fade away, leaving "reason, righteousness, and history as embodied in constitutional formulas." (as quoted in Farr 2006 p.234) History showed there was no such things as natural rights or popular sovereignty. Dunning's student Charles E. Merriam from the University of Chicago wrote *New Aspects of Politics* (1925), and saw Dunning and his colleagues at Columbia and Johns Hopkins as having "laid the foundations of modern methods of scientific political inquiry." (as quoted in Farr 2006 p.235) Along with George

Cambridge School

Catlin they argued for a naturalist image of science that became widespread.

Positivism was skeptical of the fantasy of a unity to society assumed by Idealists, and promoted the view of representative democracy as a pluralism of conflicting interests. Merriam argued that the image of democratic unity which had supported popular sovereignty was becoming harder to reconcile with the realities of American politics. It came to be harder to theoretically account for democracy in America. American politics was a conflict of group interests defining representative democracy. These could be divisive and some groups were downright anti-democratic. Walter Lippman (1921, 1925) went so far as to deny there was such a reality as public opinion or even a natural identifiable public. Harold Laski (1917, 1919) coined the term 'pluralism' in his critique of the idea of the state as a centralized authority.

The philosophies of positivism and pluralism were further articulated and formalized by Pendelton Herring

6

(1929) and George Sabine (1923, 1930). All societies are made up of several groups seeking their own self-interest. Majorities are merely an identifiable aggregate of individual preferences and only democratic insofar as they could vote for new elites. This meant there was a need for compromise and adjustment. Government has to act as an umpire and intervene when needed. To be authoritative, science must remain aloof from politics and claim ideological neutrality, even while it is assuming a particular vision of democracy. Sabine was famous for *A History of Political Theory* (1937) which told the story of the progress of liberalism developing into the American democratic polity. It showed the United States was indeed democratic, and it distinguished this from the totalitarianism of communism and fascism. What characterized democracy was not any absolute doctrine but a commitment to toleration and diversity with institutional procedures for settling conflicts. Sabine agreed with Hume's idea that one could not derive an 'ought' from an 'is.' Political science must be value free because it is incapable of justifying values. Past political theories are not exactly true because they evolved with institutions and are relative to their context. While Sabine warned of the danger of transcendental perspectives, he believed in the progress of ideas and institutions. Sabine underwrote the methodological and democratic values of political science. In 1948 Herring became president of the Social Science Research Council which funded the empirical study of political behaviour. Liberalism was reified and became supplied with a philosophy and history that was re-imposed on American politics and its development, such as in the work of Louis Hartz (1955). However, by the nineteen fifties liberalism had become a contested term.

Behaviouralism

Behaviouralism developed in the fifties in a self-conscious way as a response of political 'science' to the criticisms faced from the German emigrees: the conservatives Leo Strauss and Eric Voeglin, the socialists of the Frankfurt school Theodor Adorno and Max Horkheimer, and the existential civic-humanist Hannah Arendt. As an alternative, the Austrian philosophers of positivism Rudolf Carnap and Carl Hemple became very popular.

Harrold Lasswell teamed up with Abraham Kaplan to produce *Power and Society* (1950). Their research was originally funded by the Rockefellar Foundation for training people how to use propaganda. For them positivism was exemplified by economic modelling. Their work became more popular than 'systems theory' or 'rational choice.' Later during the 60s, this would lead to criticism of the connection between the American Government during the cold war and the American Political Science Association.

David Easton wrote *The Political System* (1953). He was behaviouralism's most articulate spokesman. He criticized the tradition for being too historicist. Too much attention was being paid to context and relativism in trying to understand past thinkers in their times and not enough to constructing a systematic contemporary theory that was both valid and useful. He said political history was unfit to train political scientists. This influenced the discipline to become more behavioural, positivist, ahistorical and turn away from normative, historical, and institutional forms of research. It resulted in an "accumulation of large amounts of empirical data, the introduction of theoretical coherence, and a clear distinction between factual and normative claims." (Gunnell 2013 p.85)

David Truman (1951) and Robert Dahl helped to popularize behaviouralism. Dahl wrote *A Preface to Democratic Theory* (1956). What distinguished democracy from totalitarianism was competitive politics where elections are the means of aggregating diverse individual's preferences and holding politicians' accountable. While multiple groups compete to advance their goals at the expense of others, they agree on the ground rules for procedures. Minorities rule through endless bargaining with an apathetic numerical majority that is never mobilized.

Behaviouralism is criticized for lacking relevance because it renounced normative concerns, and its pretence at objectivity and neutrality is undermined by a pluralist account of liberalism. They were also criticized for abetting quietism during the crises of the sixties. Political science could not be as objective and neutral as behaviouralism pretended to be because the issues it dealt with were controversial. It came with an ideology it could not openly acknowledge; pluralism was seen as a fact not an interpretation. Behaviouralism, in assuming the dichotomy of fact and value postulated by instrumental reason, believed it could only justify constitutional means to arbitrate inherently conflicting incommensurable claims, a scientific method of liberalism. As MacIntyre said of the Enlightenment project, instrumental reason ends up in a stalemate of emotivism beyond which it can't argue.

Post-Positivism

The positivism of political science was what Lipsett's criticism was really directed at, not analytic or linguistic philosophy itself. The logical positivists setup a rigorous criterion of intelligibility that was too strict. They couldn't even verify the verification principle, which said only statements empirically verifiable through the senses are cognitively meaningful, or else they are tautologies, true purely by definition, truths of logic. This threatened to reduce ethical systems to nonsense. The only metaethical positions compatible with positivism are anti-realism, where ethical statements are neither true nor false, and Mackie's error theory, where morals are lies to control the masses. Supposedly science teaches us that we live in a neutral universe. John Gunnell (2013) gave a good rundown on the history of Behaviouralism's homegrown attempt to create a positivist political science in America, which is what really undermined the creation of political philosophy until John Rawls' *A Theory of Justice* (1971).

However, a proceduralist interpretation could assume a kind of antirealist metaethics, where the decision procedure itself constructs what the good is rather than finding and discovering a pre-existing substantive value.

In *How to Do Things with Words* (1962) John Austin undermined positivism by showing you can do more with language than just make truth claims. You can perform all kinds of speech-acts that contain their own standards of felicity. In saying something, someone is also doing something in saying it (the illocutionary force), and not just because of saying it (the perlocutionary effects). Locution is the utterance itself. Illocution is the speech act performed, and perlocutions are the act's effects.

In *The Structure of Scientific Revolutions* (1962) the analytic philosopher Thomas Kuhn replaced the positivist theory of science by showing it to be a social practice, involving sudden paradigm shifts and revolutions that reinterpret everything rather than just a routine accumulation of empirical details. Paradigms are not only examples of excellent work but also determine which questions demand answers. Anomalies accumulate until a new theory is offered that resolves the apparent paradoxes. If a tradition can adapt and overcome its previous limitations, then that proves its ability to survive. This is an open question, as long as a tradition survives it can meet an epistemological crisis that it may fail to resolve, and which can put an end to its continuing relevance. A description of an observation must assume the terms of a theory and cannot be viewed without such specialist jargon. This brings us to the incommensurability of rival theories; an observation may not be capable of being translated into another paradigm. There has been a controversy over whether Kuhn was in fact a realist or a relativist?

'New realism' has overcome positivist skepticism. In 'Meaning and Reference' (1973/2000) Hilary Putnam used a causal theory of reference, rather than the descriptive one used by positivism which leads to nominalism and anti-realism. According to the description theory if we use different definitions we are talking about different things. According to the causal theory we can refer to the same thing using different theories. The reference is not an idea in one's head but the object to which you are referring. However, the different sciences view things from the perspectives of the different questions they find interesting, and according to Putnam there is no view from nowhere. This started the trend of 'new realism' in analytic philosophy.

2: The Cambridge School's Philosophy of History

Quentin Skinner

Critique of Leo Strauss

Quentin Skinner wrote 'Meaning and Understanding in the History of Ideas' (1969) as a critique of Leo Strauss, who since the fifties was the reigning theorist of the history of political philosophy. The main problem for the historian is they may find what they expect to find in a text, while the author may not have countenanced what the historian says they were doing. Alien elements can be dissolved into a misleading familiarity.

1. One misconception is for the historian to expect an author to have opinions on all the traditional issues they did not address. Strauss thought Machiavelli

showed his malicious intent by not discussing natural law. Scattered and incidental remarks may be portrayed as an author's doctrine on an expected theme, or because of some chance similarity of terminology an author may be seen as contributing to an argument they never had in mind. We could too readily find expected doctrines in classic texts. If the author meant to articulate the propositions they are being credited with, why did they not do so more clearly so the historian wouldn't have to guess at it. The historian can mistakenly praise works for being prescient of our present way of thinking, or blamed for not producing a recognizable doctrine the historian thinks they should have mentioned. This is misreading.

2. The historian may give an author more coherence than they achieved. A common strategy is to read classic texts over and over again until the reader

achieves a gestalt of coherence. The language often used is one of effort, or a quest to arrive at a "unified" interpretation. If the author's aims and successes are too various, they can be criticized for a lack of system. Statements that don't cohere with the rest of the author's thought will often be ignored, and any contradictions found rationalized into a coherence the author never had. The idea that a contradiction is a change in thought is similarly dismissed. Strauss excused any blunders by a master of writing, as the result of persecution forcing the author to hide their thoughts from the rabble. If someone doesn't find the message between the lines, they can be accused of careless reading. If the author never intended to achieve coherence they should not be criticized for not achieving it. Since concepts change over time what an author said about his work can be misleading. To say Hobbes was in reality pious, one would have to explain why his contemporaries saw the opposite. Why did Hobbes not retract or correct the offensive or misleading passages? If we are to doubt a text means what it seems to, this can only be decided with information outside the text which involves interpreting their context. Reading a text over and over again will never determine what a controversial passage actually means.

3. Finally, Skinner criticizes Strauss' idea that the tradition of political philosophy is defined by timeless perennial questions. Describing the significance some text has for our time would be easy without analyzing what the author meant to say in their time. The persistence of particular expressions tells us nothing about the persistence of questions. When we see no determinate ideas to which authors contributed, but only different agents with different intentions, we can see there really is no history of ideas but only a history of

various uses with various intentions. Authors not only answer questions in their own way, they use different jargons from different theories in such divergent ways that no stable concepts can be found. Any statement inescapably embodies a particular intention on a particular occasion and was addressed to solve a particular problem. It was inescapably specific to its context. This was the basis for the title of a series of anthologies called Ideas in Context that began publication in 1984. "There are only individual answers to individual questions, and potentially as many questions as there are questioners." (Skinner 2002 p.88)

Speech Acts and Interpretation

For the fourth series of *Philosophy, Politics and Society* (1972) Quentin Skinner wrote "Social Meaning' and the Explanation of Social Action' to critique misconceptions of both the hermeneuticists and positivists. He used John Austin's theory of speech-acts to explain the historian's project. In saying something, someone is also doing something in saying it, and not just as a result of saying it. This is the illocutionary force as opposed to the perlocutionary effects. To decode the meaning of an action is to understand the illocutionary act performed by the speaker, or the agent's intent in performing the action. Many intentions can be performed by the same action. Such an analysis can even decode non-linguistic or non-ritual actions.

Re-describing an action as an agent's intended illocutionary force can explain certain features of their behaviour. Such a re-description presents the 'point' of an action. Re-describing a policeman's behaviour as a warning removes an observer's confusion by offering an explanation. To explain the illocutionary force in a text is to explain an act in a way that does not have to refer to motives previous to the act. To decode the conventions governing the illocutionary force of an utterance is not a causal explanation, but points out certain features of the policeman's action. It is not an independently specifiable condition the way a causal explanation is. To offer a non-causal explanation is not to deny that causal explanations can offer further explanations of the same action. It may be necessary for filling in some of the background needed to understand an action.

In 'Motives, Intentions and Interpretations' (1972), Skinner explained that meaning is something prior to an author's text, but intention is something inherent in a text and cannot be expressed or performed in any other way. To explain the illocutionary force in a text is to explain an act in a way that does not have to refer to motives which are previous to the act. For the historian to recover the intentions in a text is not to identify the ideas in an author's head. An author may not fully understand their intentions and may be incompetent to state them. Machiavelli was refuting the tradition and this illocutionary force was his intent, which is not the same as the motives that prompted him to write, like securing patronage. To the extent intentions are intersubjective they are public. Gaining uptake of an illocutionary force is to understand what a speaker is *doing* in saying what they do. This is not the same as enquiring about how effectively they accomplished what they intended to achieve. This is the perlocutionary effect they have on others, and questions about the effect a text has on a reader does not have to involve the author's intent. Whatever intentions an author has, they have to be conventional to the extent they are recognized as contributing to a particular position or topic. The historian needs to know the nature and range of things that could recognizably be done with a particular statement to see what innovation an author managed to accomplish.

Skinner further developed his speech-act theory in in response to some questions raised by Charles Taylor on the status of truth in historical narrative. 'Reply to my Critics: On Meaning and Speech-Acts' is in *Meaning and Context: Quentin Skinner and his Critics* (1988) edited by

James Tully. This was later renamed 'Interpretation and the understanding of speech acts' (2002). The intention to perform a successful act of communication is publicly legible. No empathy is required because meaning is conventional. It is public and intersubjective. We may never know for sure what an author meant beyond doubt, as a final self-evident or indubitable truth; we can only have inferences from the best available evidence. A sceptic insists on too strict an account of what it is to have reasons for our beliefs. We can always construct a reasonable hypothesis. Debates about interpretation are endless, not because there is nothing determinate to be said, but because there can always be more the text says that can be fruitfully developed.

Skinner distinguished between illocutionary force and an illocutionary act. The first is a resource of language, the second is the capacity of agents to exploit it. Acts are identified by our intention, while forces are determined by meaning and context. We would be more secure that an author performed a specific act if we knew they had a motive to do so. If they had the appropriate beliefs we can examine their coherence, and if we uncover such a network of attitudes we can rest assured he intended to have exactly that force.

What connects the illocutionary dimensions of language with illocutionary acts are the intentions of the agent. An agent must not only issue a particular utterance with the form and force of a warning. It must at the same time be meant to be a warning, and be taken as a warning by being recognized as such a convention. Speech-acts are not so much a theory as a description calling our attention to a resource of language we use all the time and need to recognize in order to understand a serious utterance. Since illocutions require shared conventions, an historian must know these conventions to know what an author was doing.

We can use all kinds of verbs to describe what we are doing in saying what we do. The problem for interpretation is that we do not always explicitly articulate this. When an author does not make clear how his text is to be taken, this can often be the result of assuming the audience understands. This is problematic for the historian who is not the author's contemporary, we can be cut off from an entire dimension of understanding. Irony may be perfectly understandable in the normal way, but there could always be some doubt about whether the speaker really meant what they said. The problem is not about meaning but about illocutionary acts. Defoe argued religious dissenters should be executed. This seems to be a recommendation, but this is not what he was doing. He was ridiculing the practice. If we do not recover his intentions, we do not know what he was doing.

An author cannot use words in whatever way they like. Acts of communication have recognizable conventions and recognizable interventions. An argument is more than a string of propositions. It is to take a stand for or against an assumption, point of view, or course of action. We need to understand why a proposition was put forward in order to understand the proposition. We need to understand why a move in an argument seemed worth making by recapturing the presuppositions and purposes that went into making it. We need to understand the question/problem to which the proposition was an answer. The suppositions of a previous period in a completely different culture need to be spelled out to appreciate the subtle nature of any changes. Not only can sense and reference alter but a speech act may perform a new attitude or assessment. A particular term can change its evaluative force over time from condemnation to neutrality to commendation, and vice versa. This both reflects social change and supplements it. Any change in our concepts changes our social world.

The best effect a history of ideas can have is to enable us to stand back from our assumptions and situate ourselves in relation to very different forms of life. We should thereby develop a more objective appraisal of rival systems of thought, gain more tolerance for cultural diversity, and enlarge our horizons in a self-critical way. We may find that what we believe can be directly questionable. The alien quality in foreign systems of belief make for their relevance. They enlarge our sense of possibility.

To recap, in defining Skinner's position we may say that to understand an action, we not only have to grasp its meaning, but its illocutionary force. Recovering illocutionary intentions is the main task of the historian. The expression and reception of illocutionary force requires shared conventions; which the historian must know in order to tell what an author was doing. To understand illocutionary intentions, we have to situate them in their historical contexts. Meticulous archival and primary research can build up factual knowledge to establish what an author intended to do, securing textual interpretations. Skinner used to think there was a fact to the matter as to correct interpretations, but later in an interview in 2002 he felt the process was never-ending.

Foucault's analysis of *Parresia*

Foucault wrote "Nietzsche, Genealogy, History" where he looked at Nietzsche's attempt at a deconstructive history of the will to power, offering some precautions against self-deception. This involved four German terms: Ursprung, Herkunft, Entstehung, and Wirklicke Historie. Ursprung is origin, behind everything was neither a timeless secret nor an essence, but a fabrication created in a piecemeal fashion from disparate alien forms. Genealogy would pay a grey meticulous attention to details and accidents that are derisive and ironic, capable of undoing every infatuation. Herkunft, or lineage, would disturb what was thought to be immobile, fragment what was unified, and show the heterogeneity of what was thought consistent. Entstehung, or emergence, is when the ruled use the laws against the strong who currently impose them, so in the end they can replace the rulers with themselves. Wirklicke Historie contrasted with traditional history in refusing the comfortable recognition of our present selves in the past. In refusing to see the present as a final accumulation of a teleological continuity genealogy would oppose with disturbing discoveries those who were smugly happy in their ignorance.

Foucault did not see power struggles as a fight for justice and higher values but merely something in which we were already engaged; there was no question of not fighting. This did not give him any foundation on which to base his critique, and did not 'justify' the critical thrust of his histories which can be viewed as ending in self-defeating irony. "And it's because of the need not to tie them down or immobilize them that there can be no question of trying to dictate 'what is to be done.'" (Foucault 1978/1996) He thought we should not give into the blackmail of either you have an answer or shut up.

Foucault's lecture '12 January 1983: Second Hour' (2010) analyzed *parresia,* the Greek word for the virtue of 'frank speech;' which was a lot more positive than his Nietschean period of 1971. Foucault was concerned to show that *parresia* was vastly different from performing a 'speech act,' which his account deconstructs.

A parrhesiast stood up and spoke truth to the tyrant and risked his life. A performative utterance requires a particular institutionalized context, an individual with the requisite status in a well-defined situation. An utterance was performative insofar as the enunciation itself effectuated the thing said. It was not an assertion because it was neither true nor false. The situation of *parresia* was the tyrant surrounded by his courtiers. In a performative the effects that followed an enunciation were known, codified, and ordered in advance. *Parresia* instead opened up an unspecified risk. A logical or empirical demonstration was not *parresia* because the academic did not take any risks.

The subject's status was not important. In a performative speech act there did not have to be a personal relation between the speaker and what was said. While a parrhesiast made a pact with themselves such that they told the truth, believed it was true, and committed themselves as the one who said it; an affirmation of an affirmation. The speaker bound themselves, as the one who spoke the truth, to the consequences of having said it. The agent of a performative speech act has to have the right status to make an utterance effective. While in *parresia* the subject's social or institutional status was not the issue, but his courage.

The courage of binding oneself to the truth was the highest act of freedom. Pragmatics looked at how the situation or status of the speaker affected the value and meaning of what was said. *Parresia* was retroactive in affecting the subject's mode of being. "By asserting the truth, and in the very act of this assertion, one constitutes oneself as the person who tells the truth, who has told the truth, and who recognizes oneself in and as the person who has told the truth." (Foucault 2010 p.68)

Cambridge School

The subject did not bind themselves to the truth in the same way whether they were seer, prophet, philosopher, or scientist in a scientific institution. Foucault particularly saw *parresia* as essential to a political setting. And, speaking truth to power, as an advisor to a prince, was a traditional genre for civic humanist rhetoric, which we will look at when we study Skinner's research on the four centuries leading up to Machiavelli. The examples and exorcizes in the tradition of rhetoric were catered to many realistically possible roles, even simply only as a citizen. Writing letters and speeches taught a marketable skill, to draft official letters or presentations with maximum clarity and persuasive force. The rhetoricians began to comment on the legal, social, and political affairs of the Italian City Republics as advisors teaching virtues and condemning vices; with routine examples people could copy and use for themselves. They were not in the extreme situation of risking their lives in telling the truth to a tyrant who might kill them.

Machiavelli reversed the ethics of this tradition. He condemned for political reasons the virtues they applauded: generosity, mercy, honesty, and loyalty. He said a prince must always appear to be good but learn to be bad when necessary; one must be a centaur half-man half-beast, as sly as a fox and as ferocious as a lion. Machiavelli's *Virtus* involved martial courage and the republican responsibility of a citizen to defend their city. An army of citizens who had outside careers and families would fight to the death for their liberty, when mercenaries would run away. Skinner argued Machiavelli had his own political morality that justified his advice: doing glorious deeds to great fame, or making sure the republic survives. This is not the anarchist amoralism of Foucault's 'popular justice', Machiavelli's full rationale is explored extensively in the next chapter contrasting Skinner's and Pocock's histories of this infamous figure.

Ethics

In 1974 Skinner wrote 'Moral Principles and Social Change.' He explained how real moral principles and political ideologies were actual historical material constraining and justifying action. Positivist hard-headed historians hold that we can never take politicians words at face value, especially when they claim high moral principles to explain their action. Professed ideals will be rationalizations that sound good and can be dismissed, dubious characters will act for reasons often inadmissible. Principles play no causal role in bringing about actions, and do not need to be a part of our explanation. Principles are epiphenomenon providing no guide to the real motives and underlying realities of social and life.

On the opposite side some historians object that public figures are sincerely committed to the ideals for which they claim to act. To explain an act is normally to cite a goal to be brought about, along with the agent's belief that the act will obtain the goal. If principles are genuinely motives, then we need to cite them to explain action. Both answer the question whether the professed ideals of politicians are the determining motives for behaviour. The hard-headed historian holds that realistically and according to common sense it is never clear that principles are ever real motives, therefore we do not need to refer to professed principles to explain behaviour.

Skinner said that even in the case of someone who never believes in their professed principles, which then never serve for motives, we need to refer to professed principles to explain action. Just because someone's professed principles may be rationalizations does not mean they play no causal role in explaining actions. People want to legitimize controversial and questionable behaviour therefore they must necessarily claim their actions are motivated by some accepted principle. Even if the don't believe in their professed principles they must act as if they did or be censured. Therefore, professed principles affect our behaviour even when they are not our motives. Any course of action will be inhibited to the degree it is not legitimized. So any principle which legitimizes some action will be one of the enabling conditions for its occurrence. In the seventeenth century capitalism was thought to be immoral. Some entrepreneurs used the term religious to describe punctuality. This increased its acceptability while also channeling it towards industriousness which in turn helped to ensure the economic system developed and flourished. Even if the early capitalists did not believe in their religious rhetoric, their principles are needed to explain how and why the capitalist system evolved. Political ideology was a reality in history, so there was a call for historians to study the history of political philosophy.

J. G. A. Pocock

Skinner's historical works say what an author was doing in the context of his time, while Pocock pays more attention to languages that develop over time. He focuses on paradigms, traditions, and languages that capture similarities and links between texts and authors. Skinner saw language as a resource to be deployed, Pocock saw the power of language to constrain thought. Paradigms or languages give authors the intentions they have, what they might say and how. Yet, Pocock also declared that languages, traditions, and paradigms are changed by what is said in them.

It is preliminary to establish in what languages a passage of political discourse was written. Languages are not unified but polyvalent structures that facilitate diverse and contrary propositions, saying different things on many levels. However, if the study of linguistic contexts is neither a necessary nor sufficient method for understanding, why should historians pay attention?

Cambridge School

Pocock was more interested in explaining his actual historical practice than philosophically analyzing concepts for their own sake.

Political Languages

As far back as 1962, in the second series of *Philosophy, Politics and Society* edited by Peter Laslett and W. G. Runciman, J. G. A. Pocock entered the essay 'The History of Political Thought: A Methodological Enquiry.' It was an attempt to fill the vacancy for a philosophy of the history of political thought. Pocock stated the purpose of the history of political thought was to look at the interrelationship between institutions/traditions and the terms with which these were expressed and commented on; as well as the uses to which these terms were put. Actors respond to each other using a shared yet diverse language context.

There are irreducibly an indefinite number of approaches an historian can take, coming from within a tradition over which they have limited control. These positions can never be reduced to a single coherent pattern, nor can they always be sharply distinguished from each other. There is a certain limit on clarity. Different authors use diverse levels of abstraction from which the historian tries to tell a single coherent story. We have the means to study the distinct functions of language and how concepts migrate from one use to another. It doesn't matter so much how abstract our generalizations are as long as the historian can provide proof that the concepts were really used by the relevant thinkers in the relevant fields at the relevant time. This enables them to interpret thought as public behaviour, rendering an author's thinking intelligible. It can be very fruitful for the historian to study the stable concepts of stable societies, how these were abstracted, criticized and incorporated back into the tradition; investigating the stereotypes by which a society does its political thinking. We can study how a theory was shaped and linked to the social reality in which an author acted/wrote.

Paradigms

In 1972, Pocock wrote 'Languages and Their Implications: The Transformation of the Study of Political Thought.' This was ten years after 'The History of Political Thought: A Methodological Enquiry' and thirteen years before his essays in the late Eighties. In this one he worked with Thomas Kuhn's concept of paradigms. Kuhn revealed the history of science as revolutions in discourse and language, which determine not only solutions to problems but which problems demand solutions. An excellent example of a scientific text sets the standards for others to follow. They designate scientific authority. The history of thought is both political and linguistic. The connections between languages and the political system are polyvalent. Any sub-community of political scientists, developed to the point of autonomy, can be asked whether their language is continuous with the wider polity or not. Because paradigms operate in several contexts simultaneously performing many functions, they prescribe many distinct definitions and distributions of authority.

A heuristic construction is not a historical hypothesis unless it is worded in such a way as to be testable. For any set of assumptions, it should be possible to show whether people's linguistic behaviour is consistent with them. Hopefully at some point the author explicitly spells these out in a second-order language. If these assumptions are only recognized later, then the paradigm may have changed enough so later writers became conscious of the conventions. The historian cannot assume what the specific referent of political speech is; this has to be left to empirical investigation. But, it should be investigated which elements of experience are being articulated, how this comes to be organized in paradigmatic language and elaborated into autonomous intellectual disciplines.

Cambridge School

One tendency to be avoided is taking the extra-intellectual or extra-linguistic as "reality." Paradigms are part of the reality they order, language is part of the social structure and not epiphenomenal. We study an aspect of reality when we look at how an idea appears more real to one person than another.

Later Essays

In the nineteen eighties Pocock wrote three essays on history within three years (1985, 1987a, 1987b). He added structuralism to the theories of speech acts and paradigms for a post-positivist linguistic philosophy. Political languages are different from paradigms in that they don't preclude other languages or paradigms. Pocock borrowed some linguistic terms from structuralism and described a feedback of interaction between *la langue*, or political languages, and *la parole*, or speech-acts. It can be more important to study the languages than the utterances performed in them; to study the feedback between *la langue* and *la parole*, rather than the response of one *parole* to another. *La langues* give meaning to the *paroles* performed in them.

Pocock further incorporated speech act theory into his analysis. Political language consists in essentially disputed propositions. To describe what an author was doing, would be to say what they were getting at and what their point was. This is their illocution. There are as many acts as languages. An author performs such an indefinite variety of speech acts in a multiple diversity of contexts it is unlikely the historian can tell a single story. It can also be asked whether a writer knew what they were doing. There can be a gap between an intention and its effect. An Author takes languages from others and uses them for his/her own purposes to innovate momentary or lasting change in the way it is used. Or, the language may continue to be used in the conventional way, nullifying or distorting the effects of an author's utterance. Changes may be either deliberate or done less consciously through an indefinite number of speech acts. It may happen over so many speech acts by so many actors in so many situations with such diverse intentions that change can be seen as occasioned rather than intended.

The first thing a historian has to do is familiarize themselves with the different political languages that were in the process of being both modified and established by speech acts. Languages are necessarily shared by more than one person and research involves an extensive reading of texts of all kinds. After familiarizing themselves with the history of a genre or tradition, the historian might know what could be uttered and how things could be expressed. Contrasting what the author might have done with what they did, the historian can reveal the innovations effected, and the messages about experience transmitted. We know more about what intentions a text did perform than about those it might have but did not.

For the historian an institutional language is easier to detect than a new one within the ordinary vernacular. A problem for the historian is to question whether the languages are really there or just in the historian's imagination. To prove otherwise would be to: show that diverse authors used the idiom to perform diverse and contrary utterances; show that the idiom was used in texts and contexts different from where they were originally found; and the authors explicitly expressed it when using them. (Pocock 1985 p.10) The greater the number and diversity of performances accounted for the better the proof. A historian would also be more confident a language was not their imagination by: showing different authors performing different acts in the same language in responding to each other; if they discussed each other's language; if the historian can form predictions that are fulfilled, or more interestingly falsified; find a familiar language in a place they did not expect to find it; and if they have excluded any and all languages not available to an author. (Pocock 1987a p. 27) Hopefully an author will comment on their languages, since these are both objects and instruments of thought. They may propose words be used in a particular way.

Idioms can facilitate some acts and inhibit others, while any act can be seen as exploiting, exploring, recombining, and challenging what can be further said and done. Political speech is practical and engaged in present necessities, but also engaged in a struggle to determine what our real needs actually are. Making for contrasting ideologies that interpret the same topic differently on many levels.

Historiography of Ideologies

As far back as 1962 Pocock wrote 'The origins of study of the past: a comparative approach' (2009) where he discussed the different ideologies of history. History seems to be conservative in being concerned with tradition, but it can also be radical. Some countries give an account of their origins in terms of myths from a 'time out of time' or a 'time before time.' Historiography begins with the question: 'what authority does the past have for the present?' England has defined its national identity through common law. This presumes an authority from an immemorial time that has been forgotten. It is thought an ancient constitution which defined the balance of freedoms and prerogative for the king, lords, and commoners from a time before recorded history that was, at first, thought to have existed unchanged. Tradition is the indefinite repetitions of an action. The Levelers thought we have degenerated from the past and need to return to it. This is a radical critique of the present based on a historical claim. But then the question arises as to why the ancient constitution is authoritative? The answer may lie in nature or reason, which is not historical, but then the resulting corruption has to be explained. Henry Spelman was able to show the constitution was of Germanic origin through studying its language. It can be shown the constitution was created in a quite different time not relevant to the present. Thus, the radical can be both historical and unhistorical. Burke argued we cannot tell the conditions in which the constitution was created, but that does not matter. English institutions have adapted the constitution through a continuity of interpretation according to changing circumstances. The conservative can alternatively argue that present conditions contain their own justifications, which may be of more recent origin, such as in 1689 after the English civil war. Thus, the conservative can also be both historical and unhistorical. What the modern age has added to these older histories is the phenomena of revolutions, where peoples can affect their own changes through secular time for some teleological purpose of a new day. Thus, there are radical, conservative, and futuristic historical/unhistorical narratives.

Its as if history was a Rorschach blot test on which we can read whatever ideology we want. However, the different professional languages used in politics form paradigms and traditions that can actually be found in historical personages and used to understand them. They shape what can be said but are also changed by what is said. Machiavelli imitated and innovated within the mirror of princes' literature by criticizing their esteemed virtues, offering his own political strategies independent of customary ethics and religion. This was scandalous, but started Modern political thought with its various ideologies.

Meta-Philosophy

After-Philosophy and John Dunn

Richard Rorty said science or local knowledge and common sense are fine as they are. It's philosophy's attempt to get underneath and found the projects of epistemology and metaphysics that create wrong-headed pseudo-problems. Rorty said the modern philosophical tradition of Descartes-Locke-Kant was trapped by a metaphor; the picture of the mind mirroring nature held them hostage. Science relies on the rhetoric of paradigms.

It can never deliver nature as it is in itself, but only nature for us under some description or some perspective. The correspondence theory of truth collapses since we cannot get outside our mind to the external world and compare them. The mind is not the mirror of nature and science is interpretation all the way down.

Rorty combined Sellar's myth of the given, that all observations are theory laden, with Quine's idea that analytic definitions are not true purely a priori independently of observations but can be contingently affected by them. There are no privileged representations such that one can have pure sense data or a statement true simply by definition and logic. These were the only two ways positivists said statements could be verified and made meaningful. For Rorty there are no noncircular arguments. There is no philosophically interesting theory of truth, which is simply a term of praise for whatever survives the community's verification procedures. The philosopher has no privileged position or skill to critique the other disciplines, and the best thing to do is to drop the tradition as a failed enterprise.

We can ask why does it matter if what we do is called philosophy or not? Foucault had asked this about 'science.' "What types of knowledge do you want to disqualify in the very instant of your demand: 'Is it a science'?" (Foucault 1980 p.85) Who do you want to 'diminish' when you say you are a scientist conducting a scientific discourse? "Which theoretical-political *avant garde* do you want to enthrone in order to isolate it from all the discontinuous forms of knowledge that circulate about it?" (Foucault 1980 p.85) When Marxists strain for Marxism to be taken as a science it does not mean it is now the rational outcome of verifiable procedures, but they are investing their discourse and those who speak it with the hierarchical power reserved for science since the Middle Ages. Foucault asked who do you want to silence by asking whether it's a science or not? We can apply the same question to philosophy. Philosophy has been called upon to authoritatively rank the epistemological standings of the various disciplines. It matters if something is philosophy because *that* is so serious, technical, and deep.

We can ask whether it matters if what we are doing is to be called philosophy or something else, say intellectual history. Lyotard said that where "philosophy is forced to relinquish its legitimation duties, … [it] is reduced to the study of systems of logic or the history of ideas." (1979/1984, p. 41) If we are not into systems of logic but rather the development of ideas, we are left studying the tradition as a genre of writings that are somewhat interconnected. We do not have to accept our present interpretation of the tradition but can critique it by looking at the past when things were not seen the same way. When we are surprised by a text contrary to our expectations this can lead us to an awareness of the assumptions we have about which we tend to forget that we have them. Instead of studying eternal and perennial problems that have always remained the same. We can look at philosophers as actors in a specific context of history and realistically study their ideas that way. The Cambridge school justifies and offers this alternative without undermining philosophy.

That the two perspectives of analytic philosophy and history can conflict is seen in both Frankena's and Edel's criticisms of Alasdair MacIntyre's *After Virtue* (1982). William K. Frankena, an analytic philosopher, criticized MacIntyre for bringing in irrelevant historical narratives. The history of ideas follows the rise and fall of concepts, while philosophy is concerned with standards of rationality and truth. If one has the right conceptual equipment one can tell what a moral theory is without seeing it as a historical development. One can also assess its status as true or false and rational to believe without seeing it as such an outcome. MacIntyre criticized the stalemate of emotivism we find ourselves in as the result of instrumental reason which said we could not argue about our ultimate end but only the best means to those ends. This was part of the failure of the Enlightenment project of justifying morality without relying on traditions specific to a people's culture. Within a given tradition our virtues had a function, now our moral terms no longer make sense as if we were speaking babble. According to Frankena this has more to do with analytic philosophy than historical narrative. Historical enquiry is irrelevant. The claim is the historicist must make use of analytic non-historical standards to evaluate rational superiority. MacIntyre does not see historicism as detracting from analytical techniques but part of the point of the narrative.

On the flip side of the spectrum, Abraham Edel criticizes MacIntyre for focusing too much on explicit theorizing, articulating concepts and the stories told by the people affected, to pay attention to actual social and institutional life. MacIntyre is also criticized by Edel for distorting the complex history of morality in favour of promoting Aristotle. While Frankena criticized MacIntyre for being an inadequate analytic philosopher with an additional and irrelevant interest in history, Edel saw MacIntyre as an inadequate social historian who needlessly drags in analytic philosophy. Both criticisms reveal a tendency to oppose philosophy to history.

In the fourth series of *Philosophy, Politics and Society* (1972) edited by Peter Laslett, W. G. Runciman and Quentin Skinner there appeared an essay previously published in 1968 entitled 'The Identity of the History of Ideas' by John Dunn. The thesis was important for saying both philosophy and history are equally important for writing intellectual history. They are both answers to different questions on the same topic. One can't be ignored for the other, each corrects the other.

History criticizes intellectual history for narrating great deeds done by reified abstractions that could not really *do* anything: e.g. science is always wrestling with theology, empiricism vs. rationalism, artifice vs. nature, and real politics vs. political morality. Philosophers complain intellectual history is unconcerned with truth and more like intellectual seed-catalogues than adequate studies of thought, when delicacy in defining ideas can be important for describing what kind of actions they were.

One can be mistaken about an event actually happening when it did, or that it was of a particular kind. It is important to study both the set of argued propositions, and the set of activities men were engaged in when making these propositions: philosophical arguments and political arguing. Philosophy maps the logic of arguments proposition to proposition, but one can be wrong about the meaning of a text both through misinterpreting what someone has said and in not understanding what they were trying to do in saying it. The latter is the province of the historian and sometimes one cannot explain what an author meant unless it is uncovered what they were doing. One may understand the words that were said without comprehending their overall meaning, such as in missing irony.

Sometimes it is misleading to think a past argument is transparent to modern sensibilities, looking at biographical or social experience might help make sense of why certain propositions seemed self-evident. Thinking is a social activity created in struggling to make coherent sense of experience. Ideas are supposed to solve problems. A text "could only be said to be fully understood if one knew the conditioning-history and the set of present stimulus conditions which elicited it." (Dunn 1962 p.90) Motives and ideologies lend greater intelligibility to complex structures of ideas as social acts, offering causal explanations stating why an argument seemed cogent or an act appropriate without using a covering law. Social causation can be explained as the performance of roles specified by a description of the general social order.

We need to raise questions about the beliefs that make actions seem comprehensible and appropriate in order to explain them. A correct identification and explanation of the premises of an argument is a basic precondition for both history and philosophy. Learning from philosophers of the past cannot be done without grasping their actual arguments, while to abstract from the context of truth-criteria in which an idea was created is to change the argument. Explaining an action is not to explain a theory's truth value. It does not really matter to the history of philosophy what an author was actually *doing*. Someone's psychology does not determine the truth of a statement.

The historian however is more concerned with what an author was really doing in writing what they did: what they intended to do, what they actually did do, and what they accomplished in doing it. According to Skinner decoding the meaning of an action is to understand the illocutionary act performed by the speaker, or the agent's intent in performing the action. We need to understand why a proposition was put forward in order to understand it, as in irony. We need to understand why a move in an argument seemed worth making by recapturing the perceived opportunity to which it was a response. Not only can sense and reference change but a speech act may form a new attitude of evaluation. Whatever intentions an author has, they have to be conventional to the extent they are recognized as contributing intelligibly to a particular position or topic. Since illocutions require shared conventions, an historian must know these conventions to know what an author was doing. This takes an extensive familiarity with the tradition and all its possible moves. Speech acts are public and their interpretation can be objectively demonstrated in the writing itself, rather than being inferred from a mind inside an inaccessible actor that supposedly predetermines the meaning of a text.

For Dunn interpretation is closing the context where we know what a speaker actually intended. The problem is a historian's experience may provide premature closure. This too readily turns a fact about the past into a fact about the intellectual biography of an historian. Studying the biography of an author should correct the biographical "insights" of the historian. Only by making our fictions explicit can we have a chance to escape them.

In the end Dunn argued both history and philosophy were needed, when kept in their respective places. Both were answers to different questions on the same subject. A correct identification and explanation of the premises of an argument is a basic precondition for both history and philosophy. Philosophers complain that historians are too loose with truth and sloppy in defining concepts. While historians have criticized intellectual history for narrating great deeds being done by reified abstractions that could not really *do* anything. Following Austin, Dunn argued that sometimes one cannot explain what an author meant unless it is uncovered what they were doing, such as in irony. Biographical or social details may offer insight into the motives and ideologies that made arguments seem self-evident or an act appropriate.

We must understand an author's argument to make their actions comprehensible, remembering that abstracting from the context in which an idea was created *is* to change the argument.

Dunn recognizes that explaining an action, however, does not explain a theory's truth value. It does not really matter to philosophy what an author was actually doing. Psychology does not determine the truth, and the history of philosophy needs to be written in response to current philosophical interests, the state of the art. In the reconstruction of intellectual enterprises, the identification of a problem, why it was a problem for the author while others were not, as well as in forming a critical assessment of their solution, we turn an enquiry into the past into an intellectual project in the present. For Skinner the most valuable part of studying the past is to reveal the biases that keep us deadlocked. Therefore, it is best to combine the virtues of both philosophy and history.

The Cambridge School does not try to replace philosophy with history and, as the examples of Skinner and Pocock show, one does not have to give up philosophy to write historically. Philosophy does not occupy an Archimedean point from which to direct what other disciplines should be doing. Philosophy is to illuminate and help articulate the assumptions and practices of History, according to the current state of the art in philosophy. As an implication of this, philosophy may direct us to be careful in certain parts of our practice, but the validity of this critique is established in the art itself. History on the other hand can correct such philosophical misinterpretations as the 'metaphysics of coherence.'

The Metaphysics of Coherence

A particular bone of contention for the Cambridge theorists was what Mark Bevir (2011) called the 'metaphysics of coherence.' They were united in seeing an imposed coherence as a false hermeneutic interpretation. Dunn saw coherence as a task to be accomplished and could fail. Skinner thought a too strict adherence to assuming a grid of coherence would falsify our historical interpretations. We should not assume an author has an opinion on all topics, that contradictions are clues to an esoteric reading, and political philosophy is a series of answers to perennial questions. These are all wrong. Pocock showed there were a variety of languages coming from all kinds of professions that said many different things on innumerable levels and it would be false for a historian to simplify enough to tell a single narrative. Related to this is the idea that language both enables us to function and constrains what we can do. The rules of languages can be changed by what we say in them.

Dunn is typical of the Cambridge School's attack on the metaphysics of coherence. Coherence cannot be assumed he said, but must be empirically investigated. The works in which a set of problems issue are an attempt at a coherent rational ordering of relevant experiences, and are only intelligible in light of this context. Coherence is a struggle and it is important to describe how men really thought rather than supply them with a coherence they never had. Incompleteness, incoherence, and instability and the attempts to overcome these are ever present. In order to make sense of a rationally ordered set of beliefs we need to account for the coherence achieved or not. In 1968 Dunn was typical of the Cambridge School in seeing thinking as a social activity, created in struggling to make coherent sense of experience and not something finished and complete. We are forever trying to overcome incompleteness, incoherence, and instability with more or less success. Motives and ideologies can lend greater intelligibility to a social act, while also offering causal explanations. We only fully understand a text when we know the conditioning-history and current stimulus. Looking at biographies can explain why certain propositions seemed self-evident, perhaps correcting our assumed familiarity about arguments of the past. Only by articulating our assumptions and making our fictions explicit can we have a chance of escaping them. For Dunn we are always trying to make coherent sense of our experiences, for which we are more or less successful. It is never finished. Coherent thinking is a social speech-act, a task to be accomplished, something we need to do.

Skinner suggested we should suspect any interpretation which assumes a metaphysics of coherence that it imposes. Where statements that don't cohere with the author's other books are ignored. Contradictions can be rationalized into a coherence the author never had, while the idea that a contradiction is a change in thought is similarly dismissed. We should also not expect an author to have opinions on all the traditional issues they did not address. Scattered and incidental remarks with some chance similarity of terminology can misleadingly be seen as contributing to an argument the author never had in mind. Again, we should not assume political philosophy is the answer to timeless perennial questions that define the coherence of an academic tradition; there are as many questions as there are questioners. Any statement inescapably embodies a particular intention on a particular occasion to solve a particular problem. It is specific to its context. Coherence is not without some importance however. In order to explain our actions, we need to raise questions about the beliefs that make them seem comprehensible and appropriate. Our explanation of such beliefs depend on whether they seem reasonable or not. If they are irrational, we have to explain them differently. We necessarily have to ask the question 'are our beliefs coherent?'

Like Skinner and Dunn, Pocock thought it should be enquired into whether an author attempted to achieve unity, and to ask by what acts performed at what moments in what contexts the text achieved a unity or not. Did the author have the will or the means to organize the text into a single utterance. Was unity conceived before, during or after the work?

Pocock (1985, 1987a, 1987b) was unique in attacking the metaphysics of coherence within the nature of language itself. Texts have multiple ways of saying different things. He sees language as both a resource and constraint. Political languages are different from paradigms in that they don't preclude other languages or paradigms. There are as many different histories as there are semantic diversities in the richness of the rhetoric. Political rhetoric is designed to reconcile men pursuing different activities with a diversity of goals and values, so any utterance performs a diversity of functions at the same time in a variety of contexts. Languages are not unified but polyvalent structures that facilitate diverse and contrary propositions, saying different things on many levels. There are many irreducible political languages that differ according to the form of social life from which they originate (law, religion, rhetoric, economics, etc.), the uses to which they are put, or the ways they are universalized into philosophical theory. Each language defines political problems and values in certain ways and not others, thereby assigning authority. Languages employed by specific communities in their professions articulate the values of various activities found in institutional practices, giving more power to those whose form of life the language reflects.

Different languages come with different referents prescribing different subject matters. Languages refer to institutions, authorities, and values, with various political, social, and historical contexts. The historian can study how inhabitants in a society conceptualized their experience, what experiences they were capable of cognizing, and what responses to experience they were capable of articulating and consequently performing. Publication makes innovations known to others. The more a text becomes publicly available the more it can be used for different purposes. Any text is polyvalent in that it can have a number of diverse ways of saying different things. Any author can take advantage of this, migrating a given pattern of speech to another context, or recombining them according to the author's capacity. The goal is to show how the languages encouraged, obliged, or forbade the speaker to write in certain ways; to show what could or could not be said by a particular language. Thereby rendering the implicit explicit.

After the historian has familiarized themselves with the different languages and levels of abstraction, they can then tell which language an author is using and at what level. Individual terms migrate from one structure to another, altering some implications while keeping others. The historian can study where some rhetoric came from and the way utterances transform each other in dialogue. This diversity of origins and functions ensures statements remain multivalent and ambiguous.

Because words are polysemic and can have many different meanings a document can reveal more than intended. An author can even mean something no modern reader would understand. The point of studying history is to show how much more is meant by a statement than we assume. That we say more than we intend is an understanding shared with Derrida and his deconstruction of the attempt to control and stabilize meaning by anchoring it onto something special in either us or the world. For instance, speech is wrongly privileged over writing because it is seen as closer to the conscious self-awareness of a linguistic agent intending to say what they want, while also having the agent present to respond to questions from others and clarify any misunderstandings they may have. Derrida also commented on the way we temporally defer unto eternity the attempt to finally and adequately define the meanings of our terms, summarizing all the innumerable uses that have affected the nuance of a word. This is never complete. Many have accused Derrida and his deconstructionist followers of willfully using a text in any way they want to further their personal agendas, particularly in ways the author would never condone. The complaint is they never even try to remain true to the text and the author's intentions.

For Pocock, the effects of an author may never be over and done with. They have a continuing posthumous impact upon later writers, the text's perlocution. An Author takes language from others and uses it for their own purposes to innovate momentary or lasting change in the way some language is used. The role of an author tends to end with publication. Texts outlive their authors. The only way for the historian to study an author's posterity is through any texts left behind by their readers. So a reader would have to be a future author. Reading a text is a complex action. Text-reader relationships are unpredictable. Readers read the text as they intend, not as the author intended. Others would use an author's language in an idiosyncratic way they would not have intended; without the author's possible prediction or control. The illocutionary speech act of an author has a perlocutionary effect on a reader, to be used in further speech acts the author could not have imagined. An author may try to limit or control their audience, writing exoterically for the commoner and esoterically for a closed circle. Going public abandons such attempts at control in order to maximize the numbers of readers. Writing not intended for publication still uses public language and performs moves and innovations within it. Narratives can always be publicly contested by others. There is always more and different that can be said; History is open-ended.

Linguistic Change for Pocock

One consequence of polysemy for Pocock is that this is the source of originality and innovation within political language. The more complex and contradictory the speech context, the richer and more ambivalent the possible speech-acts, the greater the chance these acts will modify and change the speech context. Language is both a resource and constraint. Positions are not created *ex nihilo* but chosen among the alternatives offered by different traditions and their languages. Paradigms give authors the intentions they have and the means of performing them, what they might say and how. We get to know different jargons by speaking them. Once we know what can be done with them, we can tell what an author attempted to do. When the historian can show what a speaker would have ordinarily said, they can go on to explain what was in fact said. The point is not to show how a thinker's ideas are foreshadowed by earlier thinkers as philosophers tend to do, but to study the relation between the worlds authors inhabited and why they wrote the way they did. Are ideas the result of historical interests or history the consequences of personal theories? Languages to some degree select and prescribe the contexts within which they are to be recognized. They do not simply reflect experience but interact with it. The trick is to see in what ways languages indicate the contexts in which they were formed and in what ways not. Just because concepts may not be isolated as *the* determining factor does not mean they played no role whatsoever. Language reflects society but is neither an exact copy nor an unmediated expression.

Since 1962 Pocock has related languages to the acts done in them that change the language. An author cannot use just any argument; their reasoning has to be seen as valid. A historian can look at how concepts were used in particular contexts. It may be questionable how much an author's actions are determined by ideology or the historical situation. There is no single one-way relation between thought and experience, between tradition and action. There are two sides to intellectual history. There is the process by which concepts are abstracted from a tradition of behaving, talking, and thinking. Then there is what happens when these concepts are used within a tradition. Thought continuously oscillates between the practical and the theoretical, between persuasion and understanding.

The history of thought involves social events of communication responding within a paradigm, events that transform our traditions as we go. There is a feedback between *la langue*, or political languages, and *la parole*, or speech-acts, that both constitutes and is constituted by experience. Languages determine the ways their rules can be changed, but these *are* changed by what is uttered in them. For Pocock enough attention has been paid to the way thought is conditioned by external factors, more needs to be given to the way thought contests given paradigms. Once the historian knows what implications different languages have, if they come across any anomalies and innovations they will be able to recognize them. The historian should be sensitive to how words are used in new ways as the result of new experiences, thereby creating unfamiliar problems and possibilities. Idioms may facilitate some acts and inhibit others, while any act can be seen as exploiting, exploring, recombining, and challenging what can be further said and done.

Cambridge School

How do literate professionals become involved in the affairs of others and oblige them to use *their* language? The question as to what an author was doing may not be answered until we know what they did to others and to the language, which may be far from what they intended. A text is not only an event but a framework for further events. We need to know what changes were made in the discourse by other's responses and counter-moves. Once someone has heard something said, they cannot undo what was said. Instead they have to reply, even to restore the challenged conventions. This registers one's awareness that something unprecedented was said. An adversary has to accept the other's language in order to debate and deny its acceptability. Words denote different things so debate goes on as to how they are to be used. The creation of a new language may happen while attempting to maintain the old one as well as by the attempt to change it

3: The Cambridge School in Practice:

Studies of Machiavelli

The Cambridge school of the philosophy of history brought philosophy back to political science. The most classic expressions of this history were in the late 1970s with J. G. A. Pocock's *The Machiavellian Moment* in 1975 and Quentin Skinner's *The Foundations of Modern Political Thought* in 1978. These two works were preceded by four important books in the 1960s. The first two were Hans Baron's *The Crisis of the Early Italian Renaissance* in 1955/66 and Felix Gilbert's *Machiavelli and Guicciardini* in 1965. Both of which deal with the Italian Renaissance. The later two were Bernard Bailyn's *The Ideological Origins of the American Revolution* in 1967 and Gordon S. Wood's *The Creation of the American Republic 1776-1787* from 1969. Both of which dealt with the republicanism of the American Revolution. There were other classics dealing with republicanism in the Seventeenth and Eighteenth

Centuries that could be considered honorary members of the Cambridge school, notably Zera S. Fink's *The Classical Republicans* (1945), Caroline Robbins' *The Eighteenth Century Commonwealthman* (1959), and Felix Raab's *The English Face of Machiavelli* (1965). Other works like Sheldon Wolin's *Politics and Vision* (1960) as well as Hannah Arendt's *The Human Condition* (1958) and *On Revolution* (1963), while important for American civic humanism, were outside and foreign to the Cambridge School.

J. G. A. Pocock

An individual's thinking is a social event of communication and response within a paradigm, as well as an historical event that transforms the tradition. Languages determine what can be said in them, but can also be modified by what is said. Paradigms set their own rules, determine the ways these rules can be changed, and establish what questions need to be answered. Languages outlive the context in which they are modified, and impose constraints on future possible innovations and modifications. The historian should be sensitive to how words are used in new ways as the result of new experiences, creating unfamiliar problems and possibilities. The goal for the historian is to show how languages encouraged, obliged, or forbade the speaker to write in certain ways, thereby rendering the implicit explicit. When the historian can show what a speaker would have conventionally said, they can go on to explain what was in fact said. Contrasting what the author might have done with what they did, the historian may reveal the innovations effected. While idioms may facilitate some acts and inhibit others, any act can be seen as exploiting, exploring, recombining, and challenging what can be further said and done. Machiavelli was unique in his use of the paradigm of *fortuna*, contrasting it with the paradigms of custom and providence. By both imitating and renewing the traditional genre of advice to princes, he initiated

Cambridge School

Modern political thought by separating politics from philosophical ethics and religion.

In 1975 just after his essay on paradigms, Pocock wrote *The Machiavellian Moment: Florentine Political Thought and the Atlantic Republican Tradition.* The Machiavellian moment is a problem of the survival of a republic in Modern secular time, and can be contrasted with the different historiographies of the Ancients and Christians. There are two processes of history, circular and linear, and three paradigms for interpreting time: usage, providence, and fortune. The issue is dealing with time as the dimension of contingency, hence the survival of a free republic.

The particular is finite and located in time and space. It has a beginning in secular time and an end. The question is how the universal makes its appearance in the unstable world. It is a problem of making the particular event intelligible, since being less than universal it is imperfectly rational. The universal is timeless and the self-evident is self-contained. The particular is circumstantial, accidental, and temporal. Narrative is less than poetry, which is less than philosophy in the contemplation of universals. Processes of change were seen by Aristotle as circular, a thing came to be then passed away into nothingness again. It was not a linear succession of one thing after another, which is open ended. The sphere as a perfect object is only analogous to human affairs that do not seem to have any particular chronological order. Christianity, however, has a beginning in Genesis, a culmination in the Incarnation of Christ, and a future redemption and return of Christ. It is more linear but does not make a succession of contingent events more intelligible. God is outside of time or present at all times simultaneously, a *nunc-stans*. Man is fallen and grace is needed to return him to God. The contingent particular was to be only important insofar as it was symbolic, it was to be seen in the light of the eternal universal. Politics *can* be seen as a timeless universal, but in the concrete it is still limited to a particular place and time.

The First Paradigm: Usage or Custom

'Usage' was the first paradigm of temporality. Sir John Fortescue (c. 1390-1479) said all human laws were either those of nature, custom, and/or statute. Natural law could be derived from reason, logically deduced from self-evident intuitive principles. The problem was only universals could be deduced from universals. It could not produce new laws fit for specific circumstances. English common law was not universal and derived from reason but was particular to the country. The only thing natural law could determine was that a law was not contrary to nature.

Custom was the unwritten law developed over time, while statutes were laid down by the authority of the king. If common law could not be entirely deduced from universal principles, by what means could they be justified? The answer was experience. Custom derived its justification from antiquity. Its justification came from pre-history in usage and did not have to be written down as a statute. Its promulgation did not have to be conscious, we either followed custom or we did not. Because English law was so old it had proven itself under various pressures to adapt to different circumstances modified by experience. The longer it was in existence the greater its presumption to be prescriptive. Experience with the law made it second nature suitable to the nature of the English people.

The only way for an individual to tell if a law was right being to compare its effect in his life through experience, then compare his judgement to others, the more the better. Custom compared many experiences over a lengthy period of time. It took a long time for experience to be justified, what was one to do if they could not wait that long? For a legislator to draft laws as well as they could they had to come as close as possible to custom. An assembly had to be called to discuss the law and see if it was compatible with the will of the people, using the experience of as many people as possible.

Experience was based on the past, prudence determined what the future might confirm. The unprecedented was a mystery insofar as it was unique and did not conform to past experience. The king had to rely on the prudence of short term benefits to create statutes that might prove acceptable over time, but the management of policy was too specific to be universalized into laws. The kings had no more reason or experience than other men. What they did have was authority which was not based on knowledge but inscrutable providence. How were men vested with the ability to create new orders so they could legislate new laws?

The Second Paradigm: Providence

The second paradigm of temporality was 'providence.' It is ironic that while the Christian doctrine of salvation ultimately made the historical vision possible for centuries it worked to deny that possibility. The Ancients saw nothing new was to be expected; time was circular and everything would be wearily repeated. Politics did not lose interest for them however. For Christians the significance of political events was to be found in eternity. Man had fallen in the past and was to be redeemed in the future. This was temporal but ultimately related to what was outside of time. The eternal agent acted in time and gave sequences in time meaning to be consummated at the end of time when we returned to timelessness. This meaning was conferred by eschatology.

Secular time was the happenings of urban, provincial, and imperial states. How was secular time related to the Divine time of redemption? Secular events could be foretold in prophecy. Instead of being unique events succeeding each other in unrepeatable sequence they formed repeated allegorical patterns that were symbolically universal. Prophecy involved the relation of universals to acts unique in time differently from philosophy. Insofar as events occurred as tokens of prophetic archetypes they had no autonomous significance. Secular history had no sense on its own.

The political event might keep its historical uniqueness while being related to salvation, but without eschatology it had no meaning. Apocalyptic prophecy could be heretical since it could assert redemption in this world and encourage overturning all forms of worldly rule for the reign of Christ and his saints. A distinction was made between the earthly kingdom and the heavenly one. The former was inescapably imperfect and not a real part of redemption. It was not to be denied that secular history was directed by God for our ultimate salvation, we just couldn't know how and it was dangerous to speculate.

The Third Paradigm: *Virtu* vs. *Fortuna*

The third paradigm of temporality was 'fortuna.' In 525 Boethius wrote *The Consolation of Philosophy* in jail waiting for his execution. It was not a political philosophy but was a philosophy of a political man. He called *Fortuna* the insecurities to which one exposed oneself when entering into politics. He put the Greek concept into a Christian context. One could be lucky, but luck could not be counted upon. Chance could not be predicted or controlled. Virtue was the ability to deal nobly with whatever fortune might send or the fortitude to remold circumstances to one's advantage commanding good fortune; a masculine active intelligence seeking to dominate a feminine unpredictability which would submissively yield to his strength or betray him for his weakness. Why would God let *virtus* be prey to *Fortuna*? Boethius' consolation was the passive contemplation of philosophy rather than the active political life.

Cambridge School

Fortune was the wheel that raised some up to power and fame and then let them down by circumstances beyond their prediction or control. The unpredictability in politics was the secular side of history and the phenomenal world of appearance and illusion, the trick was to see it as the operation of grace leading to our salvation. Fortune for the pagans was malignant and irrational, but for the Christian believer it was providence. God perceived and directed all time at once, what we took to be misfortune was misperceived by mortals that did not share God's vision of our ultimate redemption. We could find consolation in that God did see it and everything was part of his plan. Fortune was a test of faith to prove our Christian virtue.

For Aristotle virtue was to take the unshaped circumstances fortune threw in our way and shape them to what human life should be, the activity of citizenship in civil life; as form was to matter. But Augustine thought we should transcend the secular kingdom. Contemplation was actually *the* activity most appropriate in the *civitas Dei* where our end was knowledge and communion with God, to glorify Him. Faith integrated suffering into the pattern of the redeemed life. But, because of the fall we still needed God's grace to return us to our perfected nature. Prophecy and apocalypse told the fate of empires in secular time. So public prophecy had to find a place in God's plan for redemption to again be made political. Otherwise history was just one thing following another without any sense.

There was no real room for explicating the succession of particulars in social and political time; all particulars had to find a place between experience and grace, which was rather limiting. This was especially problematic when the problem of an actual republic's fragility and instability was forced upon the mind of its citizens.

The Prince

In *The Prince* Machiavelli turned his attention to heroic individuals, the innovators who imposed *virtu* on *fortuna*. The book classifies distinct types of principalities in relation to fortune. This was Machiavelli's innovation within the traditional paradigm of *'fortuna.'* A hereditary prince is legitimized by tradition and custom, the paradigm of usage. People are used to his lineage and unless an accident happens, or he imprudently violates ancestral conventions, he does not need extraordinary *virtu* to hold on to his estate. Even if he is overthrown if the usurper makes a mistake it is easy for the former to regain their position. When ancient usage is missing *virtu* and *fortuna* become crucial. In the medieval world tradition and custom legitimized rulership, but in Machiavelli's Renaissance he faced the problem of a new prince lacking legitimacy.

By innovating a new regime, the prince makes enemies and those who welcome him may ask for more than he can deliver. It offends some and disturbs all. The people have not yet had time to get used to the new prince so that old injuries and disappointments have not been forgotten. Friends are lukewarm because they do not know what they have gained and have not had enough experience of their benefits. Biding one's time is not an option, since who knows what time will bring? *Virtu* was the instrument of innovation that exposed him to *fortuna*, while it was also *virtu* that controlled *fortuna*. The more a prince could rely on the habitual legitimacy of his predecessor the less he needed to rely on luck, but the more he needed to rely on things outside his control the more he was prey to fortune.

A hereditary monarchy or aristocracy did not much need extraordinary *virtu*. If a prince is an established monarch adding to his territories this is helped by similarity in language, laws, and customs. As long as he keeps the same laws and taxes, a change in lineage should not create much fuss especially if the old family is exterminated. Tradition will facilitate a new allegiance. If the unfamiliar territory is different in language, laws, and customs Machiavelli recommended living there. A monarch among an old aristocracy is insecure because they can always conspire, the people are loyal to them, and there are too many to exterminate. If the additional territory is an old customary republic, the prince is especially in trouble since the people will remember their old freedoms and desire revenge. They have known the realization of their true natures.

When men are no longer guided by habitual legitimacy the prince is vulnerable to unpredictable and unmanageable contingency, or *fortuna,* but since men are self-serving their behaviour can be predicted and strategically maneuvered. *Virtu* not only manages fortunes in a delegitimized world and is that which exposes the prince to fortune, but it is also what puts legitimacy into a world that has never known it.

Machiavelli turns to a private individual from inside the society becoming a new prince. The more they rely on their own *virtu* the less they are susceptible to fortune. But the more one tries to take on an already formed society the more this is a part of their *fortuna*. The ideal types who have become rulers through entirely their own virtu and not *fortuna* are the 'legislators' who created a new society like Moses. The only thing they owed to fortune was opportunity, *l'occasione*, which gave them matter to be molded into any form they thought good. The Jews had to be Egyptian slaves to follow Moses. The legislator imposes the form of a constitution upon the matter of the social body which has to have had no previous form. Unless the people were in a condition of complete anomie *virtu* would not have total independence from *fortuna*. Under the paradigm of providence, Moses saw God as the only one who could put form on formless matter. The Greeks and Romans did not have God so their legislators were demi-gods. Only prophets were inspired and authorized to innovate a whole new society.

Savonarola who inspired the Florentine republic of 1494 was executed four years later when he angered the Pope. Machiavelli said he was a prophet without a sword. Only armed prophets like Moses succeeded because he did not have to rely on goodwill but could compel men when they ceased to believe.

What about the new prince whose *virtu* is not independent of *fortuna*? A prince that owes his position to nothing but luck would soon be disposed. What is interesting is a person who can counteract their initial dependence on fortune. Machiavelli's example was Cesare Borgia. He only got a chance because his father was Pope. But he gained such a hold over Romagna before his father's death that he was able to hold onto his position. His father gave him the *occasione* to use his *virtu* to become independent of *fortuna* before she could turn the wheel against his favour. What was at risk was not the

Romagna's reaction, offending more than he attracted, but to make sure his military power might outlive the fortune of his father's unpredictable demise. Such a new prince did not impose form on the formless like a superhuman legislator creating a new society. He altered old forms and established a *stato* (the state as a limited form of government, only partly legitimized and partly rooted in customs new to the people) which needed more extraordinary *virtu* than a legislator.

The sole purpose of the new prince was to maintain his state. The new prince, however, cannot hope to achieve the long-lasting stability of a hereditary heir or a legislator. He must keep a watch out for short term immediate dangers. Internationally, to fend off competition from other princes he must raise a citizen army, not mercenaries, and spend all his time learning the skills to use them properly. Domestically, because of his innovation the prince lives in an environment only partly legitimized and subjected to morality. *Virtu* is knowing when to act morally and when not. The wisest course was to act aggressively so as to be feared, since love takes more time. With the world so unstable after innovation, the unexpected is a constant threat, to act in time was to impose form on *fortuna*. No *virtu* can make the same strategy work all the time, nor can it entirely make us flexible enough to change our nature in time to avoid all chances of ruin. Without the stability of an established republic, only the short term view could prevail.

Comparing the three paradigms in *The Prince* we may say that each paradigm excludes the others. Both a hereditary heir and a divine legislator are not in the same situation as a new prince having to use his *virtu* to combat *fortuna*, the subject of *The Prince* dedicated to Lorenzo de' Medici the new ruler of Florence.

A hereditary prince is legitimized by tradition and custom, the paradigm of usage, he does not need extraordinary virtu. When men are no longer guided by habitual legitimacy the prince is vulnerable to unpredictable and unmanageable contingency, or *fortuna*.

For a new prince coming from inside the society, the more they can rely on their *virtu* the less susceptible they are to *fortuna*. But the more a society is already formed the more this is a part of *fortuna*. Legislators who create a new society like the demi-gods Romulus and Remus who founded Rome, or Moses who followed God who he thought was the only one who could put form on the formless masses, the paradigm of providence. Machiavelli thought only armed profits succeeded because they could compel men when they ceased to believe.

A new prince whose *virtu* is not independent of *fortuna* does not create a new society but modifies old forms to established the state as a limited form of government. Because of his innovation he lives in an environment that is only partly legitimized and moral. *Virtu* is knowing when to act by the rules and when not.

With the world so unstable after innovation the unexpected is a constant threat and to act in time is to impose form on *fortuna*. *Virtu* can't make the same strategy work all the time, nor can it make us flexible enough to change in time to avoid ruin. A new prince cannot hope to achieve the long-lasting stability of a hereditary heir or divine legislator. He must stay ever vigilant, alert to the short-term immediate dangers of *fortuna*.

The three paradigms of usage, providence, and *virtu* vs *fortuna* are mutually exclusive. A new prince susceptible to *fortuna* is not a hereditary heir legitimized by custom, nor a divine legislator imposing form on the formless. He is more in constant danger of losing his state and must adapt to the changing times. *The Prince* was written for this situation. The environment that inspired Machiavelli's radical advice when compared to our times was quite unstable and barbaric, we've had a well-established rule of law and public accountability for centuries now. In 1969 Gordon S. Wood published *The Creation of the American Republic 1776-1787* which covers the debates from *The Declaration of Independence* to the ratification of the Constitution. Two hundred and forty years is a long time for a republic. Electing a new president is routine. We may not be as prey to *fortuna* as Renaissance Italy, but luck still has the ability to raise some up and bring them down, and we still have to deal with unexpected contingencies in the rest of the international world. So the paradigm is still relevant, while muted.

Quentin Skinner

Quentin Skinner said a common strategy is to read classic texts over and over again until the reader achieves a gestalt of coherence the author may never have had. Reading a text over and over again can never determine what a controversial passage actually means. If we are to doubt a text meant what it seems to, this can only be decided with information outside the text, which involves interpreting its context. This involves an extensive reading of texts of all kinds. The social context is the framework of conventionally recognizable speech-acts possible for an author to have intended. Any statement inescapably embodies a particular intention on a particular occasion and was addressed to solve a particular problem. It is inescapably specific to its context. The context is the history that forms the background for a text. Skinner describes the development of Renaissance republican literature over four hundred years. Showing that Machiavelli's work did not come from nowhere *sui generis*, he shows where and how he was truly innovative. The development to Machiavelli took four hundred years of changing fashions in the study of rhetoric which were not unified by perennial questions. By studying the tradition that formed the background to Machiavelli, Skinner is able to show what speech acts he was actually trying to perform and this helps us understand nuances of his philosophy.

The Dictatores

The ideology of republican liberty came from the teachings of rhetoric in the early twelfth century. The basic goal of the *Ars Dictaminis* was to teach rhetoric and this was accompanied by a wealth of examples, mainly letters. The purpose being to compose documents with clarity and persuasive force. The *dictatores,* teachers, turned from using pie in the sky examples to ones that could actually be used by professionals. In this way they turned to issues of legal, social, and political affairs. By the early thirteenth century oral speeches were added, the *Ars Arengendi.* Thus rhetoric became even more important for public politics and law and the *Ars* were use to directly comment on civic affairs. Two genres developed. The first was city chronicles. Instead of using history to illustrate divine providence, speech and letter examples were used to illustrate propaganda and events. An example would be to exhort people to take up arms and fight for republican liberty. The second genre was advice books for *Podesta* and city magistrates. These abandoned the pretence to teach rhetoric and presented the *dictatores* directly as political advisors. These books offered lists of virtues to be cultivated and vices to be avoided.

The Classical Humanists

A humanist form of theory was introduced to Italy from France by the second half of the thirteenth century. It used classical authors as examples of high rhetorical excellence. Before rhetoric was no more than a practical business course. Poems and the works of Cicero became the main sources for inspiration. In the early fourteenth century lawyers began to study the ancient poets and historians not only for their usefulness but as great works for their own sake. Histories modeled after Livy's and Sallust's were produced. Uniting Cicero with Aristotle it was seen there was a link between speaking and governing well. The influence of the classics was to promote greater sophistication with greater confidence and more systematic arguments, which helped develop an ideology of republicanism in the face of the tyranny.

Right off one of the reasons for the demise of republican liberty and the rise of despotic tyrannies was the presence of factions between the old and new rich. Another reason was the rise of private greed that undermined the virtues and the public good, and which also led to factions. People must set aside selfishness and identify themselves with the good of the city. Good institutions are not enough to make men virtuous, but if men are virtuous then the health of institutions are secondary. Everyone should be able to hold offices. The only true nobility is one of virtue. The lineage of a great name and wealth pales in comparison. Virtue is an individual achievement, not the property of a family. The rhetoricians did not pay much attention to administrative structures but focus on the genre of advice to princes. A prince must truly have virtue. Appearance, pretence, and semblance will not secure their continued governance. He must also be generous with his pay to secure loyalty. Miserliness is horrible. It is better to be loved than feared and to be merciful than cruel if one wants to survive. Also, it is important never to lie and commit fraud. One cannot win honours by trickery or force. One should at all times practice virtue and should be ashamed to degrade themselves by practicing vice. Cicero said one should always be an upright man and never lower themselves to being a beast with the ferocity of a lion or the cunning of a fox.

Civic Humanists

Hans Baron's account of the sudden rise of the highly productive period of republican literature in Florence at the beginning of the fifteenth century did not give enough credit to the inheritance of the City Republics of medieval Italy and the influence of Petrarch (1304-1374). There were similarities and differences between the *dictatores* and the later humanists. They shared a legal education that led them to teach rhetoric at the Italian universities or serve as secretaries for the cities or the

Church. They both were concerned with the corruption of republics.

While the *dictatores* blamed factions and private wealth, instead the civic humanists blamed the use of mercenaries. The humanists saw liberty as both freedom from external interference and the ability to partake of running the commonwealth. This was not something new but came from diplomatic negotiations, city chronicles, and political propaganda as far back as the middle of the thirteenth century. Both preferred republicanism over monarchy. Kings were suspicious of virtue in anyone but themselves, while republics promoted virtue in everyone.

Leonardo Bruni added that honours available to everyone would lead men to develop their talents to the uppermost. This was derived from the *dictatores* assumption that personal virtue was more important than the machinery of government. Bruni added that in Florence men preferred public service to leisure. The later humanists also held that virtue was the only true nobility.

Individual self-development was more important than good fortune. In History the civic humanists followed the scholastics in favoring the Roman Republic over the Empire. According to Bruni, it's greatness was due to the opportunity everyone had to take part in the government. When this liberty was taken away Rome became corrupt and was taken over by Caesar.

With the classical humanists many texts were uncovered that had to do with Ancient history, poetry, and morality. In the middle ages Greece and Rome were seen from the light of contemporary concerns. Instead the humanists came to see the Ancient world as separate and a world unto its own. Petrarch came to see Cicero not from the lights of the *Ars Dictatores* but as having his own goals of education. Virtue or *virtus* came from *vir* which meant 'man.' The goal of education was *vir virtutis*, or to create a manly man that united wisdom and eloquence, so the truth was effectively communicated and philosophers influenced public affairs. It was possible to achieve this highest excellence with the right education that combined rhetoric with Ancient philosophy. The scholastics may know from Aristotle what the good was but without eloquence the teacher could not inspire the student to go after it. Only rhetoric combined the practical with theory.

A new genre arose that gave advice not only to *Podesta* or princes but on what formed the best education. History was most important followed by morality and then rhetoric. In the high Middle Ages there was one kind of education for the gentleman who read Aristotle, and another for the clerks who studied chivalry and the arts of war. With the civic humanists the two were ideally to be combined. In the Middle Ages Augustine thought man was so sinful that we could only obtain a hint of virtue by the grace of God alone. Virtue was not achievable by man by himself and it was subsequently dropped from discussion. Petrarch was not pagan but Christian. He said the virtuous man not only acquired each of the four cardinal virtues but the three holy virtues as well. Wisdom was piety.

They disagreed however with Augustine's account of our fallen nature. A new genre extolled the excellence and dignity of man. Since such heights were possible, it was our duty to obtain them. Such optimism saw we could shape our own destiny and remake the social world as fit our desires. Fortune turned the wheel of our fate rising some up and bringing them low. But fortune favored the brave and could be wooed and subdued by true *virtus*. Augustine thought to worship Fortune was to deny providence, and God's plan was not susceptible to man's will and virtue.

The humanists may have pessimistically felt the overriding tyranny of Fortune over providence, but they also believed we could become masters of our fate and perform the greatest deeds. The dignity of man lay in his God given free will. Introspection became a new fad of exploring our natures. Discovering the secrets of nature so that we could use our environment became a new attitude, as did the increasing value of work. The great reward for *virtu* was praise, glory, fame, and honour; having an immortal name that lives on. Augustine saw living for praise as vain. However, the humanists were Christian enough to think virtue was its own reward, and vices were to be avoided simply because they were evil.

Even though the fifteenth century civic humanists developed a tradition that came before them, why did they see the praise of republicanism as the appropriate response? It was because they wanted to patriotically defend the liberties of Florence against the threat of Visconti, Duke of Milan. Also important was the rivalry with scholasticism. They criticized the methodology of Bartolus who thought Roman law should supply answers to contemporary questions. Rome was an alien world that should be studied on its own terms. The civic humanist's alternative was historical jurisprudence with a comparative study of different legal systems. They also criticized the abstractness and remoteness of scholasticism arguing that philosophy should be of practical use for social and political life. Instead of trivial quiddities they thought we should study how to live. When the scholastics did study society they were content to multiply useless distinctions when it was better to will the good than know the truth. All knowledge was to be useful, so the humanists promoted experimental sciences and practical arts like architecture. Public service was more valid than solitary contemplation. Correspondingly the civic humanists tried to address all of their neighbors and citizens rather than just magistrates and *Podesta* like the *dictatores*. Along with the attack on scholasticism came a new vision of History. Augustine saw history as a linear march of God's plan. The later humanists saw that time was cyclical. They agreed with Ecclesiastes that there was nothing new under the sun and history repeated itself. They came up with the term the 'Middle Ages.' They saw the Ancient world was replaced by the dark ages of barbarism, despite the Incarnation. Their own age was a Renaissance or rebirth and return to life and light. They might even surpass the Ancients.

Mirror-for-Princes Literature

Almost as soon as the republics were born they were taken over by tyrants or *Signori*. This affected the political literature at the end of the fifteenth century and the turn of the sixteenth. The life of civil service faded and the life of leisurely contemplation grew in prominence as the idea of meaningful involvement came to seem impossible. Politics came to be seen as a vulgar form of intellectual pursuit, and Plato was held in higher esteem than Cicero. It used to be that the humanists addressed all of their countrymen but focus shifted to the princes, and perhaps their courtiers - as a new extension of the genre. Many books of the called the mirror-for-princes literature were written for and dedicated to specific princes.

The most (in)famous was Machiavelli's *The Prince*. Machiavelli dedicated *The Prince* to Lorenzo de Medici, from whom he was hoping for patronage, possibly a paying post. It was still assumed the prince should use *virtu* to win honour, glory, and fame – to be renowned for great deeds. Machiavelli thought the Medici's could gain glory by founding a new principality with new laws and new institutions. Crimes could bring power but not glory. It was still thought that what laid waste to most plans was unexpected fortune that could do irreparable damage. Machiavelli said a prince could gain their position by luck or *virtu*. One should rely on one's own *virtu* rather than luck which will abandon you when you most need it. A prince with true *virtu* will never be dominated by luck but be able to use it to their advantage. Machiavelli thought fortune controlled half of what we do but the other half is ours and fortune favors the brave and audacious. We must rely on our own actions.

A classical education in both humanities and war should still be the first duty of the king and courtier. (Machiavelli was less concerned with this.) There were some changes from what came before. Liberty and justice used to be the main values in political life. These were replaced with security and peace. Liberty was licence rather then living by good laws. Machiavelli thought subjects could be stabilized and secure under the control of a prince that looked after their security, strength, and longevity.

It was thought princely *virtu* involved all four of the cardinal virtues and the three theological ones. The early humanists wrote for *Podesta* or magistrates and talked about virtues specifically meant for rulers. This had been dropped by the civic humanists who wrote for everyone. Generosity for patronage, like founding public buildings such as theatres and churches, were a path to glory. Miserliness was to be avoided as demeaning and shameful. The prince was to display mercy and not cruelty which was disgraceful. The prince would be more secure and live longer if they were loved rather than feared. Liberality and clemency were the two most important virtues. Also of note was exceptional scrupulousness in always telling the truth and never breaking one's promises.

Machiavelli's first contrast with the mirror-for-princes literature was that he saw power as essential not just virtue. Persuasion must be supplemented with military force, an economy of violence. With good arms good laws follow. Also like the civic humanists he thought we must have citizen armies of our own rather than use unreliable mercenaries.

Machiavelli was also original in denying the prince must always have all the virtues. Sometimes one must be cruel to be kind. Being generous can lead a ruler to impose burdensome taxes which subjects resent, and it can be better to cruelly set some examples to save bloodshed later on. What is important is to seem and appear to have the virtues all of the time. Men being simple and self-interested will always be willing to be duped. As long as people do not get too close one's acts will be judged by their results. One must be prepared to not be good when fortune deems it necessary. The gap between how one lives and one should live is so great that if one always does what one is 'supposed' to they will come to ruin. One should break one's promises when to do otherwise would lead to a downfall and threaten the life of the country.

To remain virtuous when so many around us are not is foolish. It is better to be feared than loved since men are so fickle they will break the bond of love when it is to their advantage, while the threat of punishment will always be effective. Machiavelli never denies that one should be good as much as possible, but one should be bad when necessary. Machiavelli did not deny the value of morality he merely had his own set of morals, such as the overriding importance of helping the prince maintain their state and do important things to great glory.

Machiavelli and his Republican Contemporaries

Skinner compared what Machiavelli had in common with his contemporary humanists. The fundamental ideal was political liberty, traditionally defined as both freedom from external interference and the ability to run the government. While *The Prince* extolled security, *The Discourses* (1517/1970) promoted liberty as of overriding importance, even over conventional morality. The primary aim of any legislator is to foresee all the laws required for the maintenance of liberty. The greatness of the Roman Republic was the creation of new institutions to support the liberties enjoyed. The expansion of the military empire helped keep Rome peaceful in its liberties. Those who thought of nothing but liberty made for a true Roman.

Everyone accordingly agreed the best form of government was republicanism. Machiavelli admitted that the corruption and decline of the state could only be reversed by an exemplary individual, not by the public as a group. However, he preferred popular government. The populace displays ingratitude more rarely, makes fewer mistakes, elects better magistrates, and in general is more prudent, stable, and has sounder judgement. A popular government is more likely to look for the good of everyone. Some contemporaries preferred the balance of power to be weighed in favour of the aristocracy who are experts in prudence. Machiavelli preferred the masses.

All humanists were concerned with what might threaten the demise of a republic. Many contemporaries thought extravagant luxuries and greed made men selfish and dishonest. The rich it seems did not esteem the virtues, and would use bribes to increase their power. Machiavelli thought poverty could bring honour to cities. Everyone agreed that the use of mercenaries brought ruin to cities, which was Machiavelli's pet peeve.

Humanists of this era gave a particular new focus on the corruption of the people, a failure to devote oneself to the common good. When people in power looked out for only their own interest they introduce laws meant to further their own power at the expense of others. Then, the people will promote licence while the nobles promote slavery. For Machiavelli corruption meant ineptitude for a free life. Dictators and generals when given a long enough rule could move armies onto their side against the common good.

Machiavelli was uniquely concerned that Christian morality left us prey to predators because humility, contemplation, and contempt for mundane things made us weak, cowardly, and unfit. Religion when used right could strengthen our love for the fatherland, but Christianity made us effeminate. Guicciardini agreed and was even more vehement.

Virtu meant preserving the life and freedom of the city and promoting the common good above everything else. When making a political decision one must be as virtuous as possible but when necessity demands one must preserve the state regardless of what is praiseworthy or not. The ends justify the means. *Virtu* could be incompatible with virtues. This scandalized all of his contemporaries, except Guicciardini.

How could we avoid these dangers? Some despaired it was impossible. The best method for finding out what led to corruption and what could save the republic was History. Machiavelli thought history repeated itself. Since men had the same passions the same consequences followed. He did not follow antiquity because it was ancient but he saw Rome as uniquely successful. *Virtu* meant civic pride and patriotism was more important than effective institutions for maintaining liberty. These writers discussed *virtu* in more general terms than the mirror-for-princes literature. *Virtu* was not only the property of princes but could be a characteristic of society in general as 'public spirit,' just as corruption could be a quality held in general. *Virtu* was the ability to put the common good above selfish interests. It enabled a free people to maintain their liberty and enhance the greatness of the commonwealth. Just as a prince maintained his state for the highest prizes of honour, glory, and fame. The mirror-for-princes literature held *virtu* was acquired by a proper classical education. Machiavelli held that good civic examples and knowledge of the affairs of the state were a good start. But the more popular answer seconded by Machiavelli came from the civic humanists, avenues for public advancement should be open to everyone and made as alluring as possible. Republicanism was the best guarantee of *virtu* and *virtu* was the best guarantee of keeping a republic alive.

One reversal from what came before was an attention given to the machinery of government over the virtues of princes. Venice was particularly esteemed. By the turn of the sixteenth century all the City Republics in Northern Italy had succumbed to the tyranny of the *Signori*. All except Venice which kept the constitution it had created in 1297. It alone kept its liberties at the same time it kept the peace. It was called the most serene republic.

In 1394 Piero Paolo Vergerio was the first to explain the stability by pointing to a passage in Plato's *Laws* that said the most sound and secure government combined monarchy, aristocracy, and democracy. The Florentine Donato Giannotti (1492-1573) published in 1540 a book that said while Venice combined the rule of the one Doge, the few in the senate, and the many in the *Consiglio Grande,* their complicated system of voting and balloting was also vital. The venetian Gasparo Contarini (1483-1542) wrote a panegyric ode to Venice that said the most important duty of its citizens was to preserve its perfect constitution from being altered. He argued factions were not a problem because each group evened the others out, smoothing conflict.

Machiavelli was the exception in that he was not so impressed. He preferred the expansion of Rome over the serenity of Venice. Machiavelli was contrary and thought civil competition and discord helped produce the best laws. There was an inevitable strife between the rich and the poor in Rome such that there was a balance that no one group would legislate too much in their own favour to the criticism and vetoes of others. Each provided a check on the other. The valorizing of conflict proved too scandalous to Machiavelli's contemporaries.

One final common theme was that *Virtu* used to be seen as possibly overcoming the tyranny of fortune. Machiavelli said there was always hope so we should never give up. As the sixteenth century neared its end it became harder to believe *virtu* could parry the blows of fate when practically all the republics collapsed. Machiavelli even came to hold that we could not oppose luck but only accommodate it. With the collapse of optimism came the end of Renaissance republican literature.

Conclusion

Is ethics good for politics? Can politics be ethical? Ethics is more the domain of philosophy, politics has it own domain with its own laws that can be studied empirically. Political ideologies are like schools of ethics. They both deal with what is considered right or wrong. Marx thought impersonal ethics were merely an idealistic cover for ideologies that were based on our class. It was a mirage for power struggles that were not in themselves ethical. In contrast, Skinner showed that early capitalists used religious terms to describe their business. To be accepted they had to consistently apply their supposed standards and ideals with strict discipline. To pretend to be religious about their business they actually had to be religious about it. So ethics and standards have their own independent weight that influence actions even for politicians, who Machiavelli had said must always appear to be completely virtuous even when not.

Pocock studies Machiavelli's politics not his ethics. Since men are self-serving their behaviour can be predicted and strategically manipulated. Politics follows its own rules. Machiavelli's new prince is not a hereditary monarch based on the paradigm of usage. In the medieval world tradition and custom legitimized rulership, but in Machiavelli's Renaissance he faced the problem of a new prince lacking legitimacy. When men are no longer guided by habitual legitimacy the prince is vulnerable to unpredictable and unmanageable contingency. If we follow the same strategy all the time, we will come to ruin when circumstances change. *Virtu* is knowing when to act morally by the customary rules and when not. *Virtu* not only manages fortunes in a delegitimized world, but also puts legitimacy into a world that has never known it. The prince is also not a new legislator imposing form on a formless mass, like a prophet following the Divine plan of providence. The religious paradigm. Separating church and state is one of the staples of modernity. Machiavelli was particularly critical of the advice of Christians for politics. Politics follows its own rules. This understanding is particularly modern and was begun by Machiavelli.

Skinner's proposed that for new groups to justify their actions to others, they had to consistently act as if they held to their values. To pretend to be virtuous one had to actually be virtuous. We can see that Machiavelli justified his wisdom with coherence and consistency when he overturned the traditional advice to princes. This involved a political/moral rationality that justified certain strategies and not others. However, Machiavelli did not especially esteem consistency. If we always reacted with the same strategy, we will come to ruin when circumstances change and the old ways don't work. The contrast between the tradition and Machiavelli can be compared virtue by virtue.

Skinner discussed Machiavelli's political criticism of virtue ethics. The Ciceronian tradition of applying virtue ethics to politics created philosophical speculation that was belied by experience. Liberality and clemency were the two most important virtues. Getting a reputation for generosity like founding theatres and churches was a path to glory; miserliness was demeaning and shameful. The prince was to display mercy and would be more secure to live longer if they were loved rather than feared. Exceptional scrupulousness was demanded in always telling the truth and never breaking one's promises.

Machiavelli never denies that one should be good as much as possible, but one should be bad when necessary. Ethics is social but also personal. If the state follows advice meant for individuals only, it will come to ruin. Being generous can lead a ruler to impose burdensome taxes which subjects resent. It can be better to cruelly set some examples to avoid more bloodshed later on. One should break one's promises when to do otherwise would lead to a downfall and threaten the life of the country. In attacking the virtue tradition Machiavelli used reasoning that was moral. It was the survival of the state that justified a seemingly amoral stance in the face of changing and unpredictable *fortuna*. Machiavelli did not deny the value of morality, he merely had his own set of political standards that put the survival of the prince or republic first. The prince could go on to do great glorious deeds to great fame, while a republic meant the people ruled themselves. In *The Discourses* (1517/1970) Machiavelli said we needed the cardinal virtues of courage, temperance, and wisdom to secure liberty and protect the republic. This is a purely classical formulation found in Machiavelli. He is different in not including justice. We need a certain ruthlessness to discount justice when necessary for the common good.

Pocock thought Machiavelli wanted to show the independence of politics from ethics/custom and religion. Skinner tried to show that Machiavelli was not actually amoral but had his own political morality. Pocock contrasted the paradigm of *virtu* vs. *fortuna* with those of usage and providence. Skinner described the four-hundred-year context that formed Machiavelli's background. Both saw Machiavelli as initiating Modern political thought in the Renaissance. His writing was in transition between the old world and the new one. This is why it is important to revisit Machiavelli again and again. He holds a key to understanding how we got to where we are. *Fortuna was* an incredibly old mythical paradigm when Machiavelli used it, but he was new in trying to contrast speculative moral philosophy with facts about sovereignty derived from examples in history. This began a new modern attitude with its own moral/political rationality that justified contrasting ideologies. Today civic humanism has been replaced by proceduralism, and needs to be retrieved historically. Hence, the importance of revisiting Machiavelli. He thought the best way to secure liberty was to have a free society not controlled by tyrants within or conquerors without. This meant a republic with plenty of public offices open to all the citizens, best served by the cardinal virtues.

4: Applications: Negative Liberty and Non-domination

In 1969 Isaiah Berlin contrasted negative and positive liberty. Negative liberty is freedom from interference, positive freedom is to be self-directing. In 1983-4 Quentin Skinner wrote two essays on Machiavelli in response. The first essay shows that a negative concept of freedom was compatible with a theory of human nature that said we needed a particular form of polity and the best way to serve this is the cardinal virtues. The second essay argued that the law can force us to respect and protect our freedom, and this was contrasted to positive liberty. These two essays influenced Philip Pettit (1997 p. 27) to think republicans did not have a positive conception of liberty. In turn, during Skinner's Inaugural Lecture as Regius Professor of Modern History at the University of Cambridge in 1997 (p. xi), he thanked Pettit for helping his research on the understanding of freedom in seventeenth century Britain, the topic of the lecture, which came to be entitled *Liberty before Liberalism* (1998). In *Republicanism: A Theory of Freedom and Government* (1997) Pettit made a distinction between interference and domination. Liberty was freedom from arbitrary domination. He argued that while the laws interfered with us that was not a great threat to our freedom, since it did not have to be arbitrary but could serve our interests in a way that respects our opinions. We can't have a law for everything, there must be some discretion, and democracy is the best way to make sure official decisions are not arbitrary. As long as we can contest the judgements of government we can make sure they are following our values and ideas.

Isaiah Berlin

Negative Liberty

Negative liberty is defining an area within which the subject is without interference from others. Beyond a certain minimum a person is 'coerced' or 'enslaved.' There must be a certain minimum area of personal freedom that must not be violated. If it is overstepped, we are in an area too narrow for a minimum development of our natural faculties, which make it possible to pursue our goals, or even conceive what our ends are. Liberty is liberty *from*. It is pursuing our own good in our own way.

The incommensurability of our ultimate values makes sure negative liberty is inescapably necessary. The right to choose trumps any substantive account of the good which is inherently going to be contestable and controversial. Tragedy, the necessity of choosing between absolute claims, is an unavoidable part of the human condition. Freedom is measured by "the number and importance of the paths they keep open for their members." (Berlin 1969/2002, p. 211) Freedom is "an end in itself, and not a temporary need, arising out of our confused notions and irrational and disordered lives, ... which a panacea could one day put right." (Berlin 1969/2002, p. 214) The freedom to choose ends without claiming eternal validity for them may drive cray those who seek for "final solutions and single, all-embracing systems, guaranteed to be eternal." (Berlin 1969/2002, p. 215) "To preserve our absolute categories or ideals at the expense of human lives offends ... the principles accepted by those who respect the facts." (Berlin 1969/2002, p. 216) Negative liberty does not "deprive men, in the name of some remote, or incoherent, ideal, of much that they have found to be indispensable to their life as unpredictably self-transforming human beings." (Berlin 1969/2002, p. 216-7)

Liberty could not be unlimited, then everyone would interfere with everyone else, minimum needs would not be satisfied, and the weak would be exploited by the strong. Action must be limited by law. Everyone must be given a minimum of freedom so others are restrained by force from interfering. The whole function of laws is to prevent such collisions. Purposes and activities do not automatically harmonize. It is seen as necessary to limit freedom for other values, even to protect freedom itself. Berlin mentions justice, happiness, culture, security, equality, love of our fellow man. I may be ready to willingly sacrifice some freedom for other values, and should be 'guilt-stricken' if I'm not, but unless our sacrifice increases the individual liberty of others it is still a loss of freedom.

Positive Liberty

Here the question is "Who is to be Master?" We want "to be moved by reasons, by conscious purposes, which are my own, not causes which affect me, as it were, from outside. ... A thinking, willing, active being, bearing responsibility for my choices and able to explain them by references to my own ideas and purposes." (Berlin 1969/2002, p. 178)

In escaping spiritual slavery there is one part of us that rules and another part that is ruled. There is a higher nature variously called reason, the real, ideal, or autonomous self. Then there is the lower nature, my empirical' or 'heterogeneous' self of irrational impulses and uncontrolled desires; the pursuit of immediate pleasures, "swept by every gust of desire and passion, needing to be rigidly disciplined." (Berlin 1969/2002, p. 179)

The higher or more real self can be something wider than the individual. "This entity is then identified as being the 'true' self which, by imposing its collective, or 'organic', single will upon its recalcitrant 'members', achieves its own, and therefore their, higher freedom." (Berlin 1969/2002, p. 179) We can coerce men to do something they would want to do themselves if they were more "enlightened." We can coerce them for their own sakes, in their interest not ours. We may justify this because we think we know what they truly need better than they do. Our 'true' selves after all can be submerged and inarticulate. They would not resist if they were rational and understood their interests as we did.

> Their 'real' self, of which the poor empirical self in space and time may know nothing or little, ... is the only self that deserves to have its wishes taken into account. Once I take this view, I am in a position to ignore the actual wishes of men or societies, to bully, oppress, torture them in the name, and on behalf, of their 'real' selves. (Berlin 1969/2002, p. 180)

The French revolution was felt as "collective self-direction on the part of a large body of Frenchmen who felt liberated as a nation, even though the result was ... a severe restriction of individual freedoms." (Berlin 1969/2002, p. 208) The point according to the liberalism of Berlin is negative liberty is compatible with the absence of self-government. What is important is the area of control, not the source. It has been argued that self-government protects rights better than other systems. But there is no necessary connection between individual liberty and democratic rule. The transformation of sovereignty from one set of hands to another doesn't increase liberty but merely shifts the burden of slavery. Why should someone care if they are "crushed by a popular government or by a monarch, or even by a set of oppressive laws?" (Berlin 1969/2002, p. 209) The main problem is not who has the authority, but how much authority should be in any set of hands. Liberty is endangered by the mere existence of absolute authority.

> "Democracy ... can still crush individuals as mercilessly as any previous ruler. ... universal consent to loss of liberty does not somehow miraculously preserve it. ... If I sell myself into slavery, am I the less a slave? ... Constant could not see why, even though the sovereign is 'everybody', it should not oppress one of the 'members' of its indivisible self, if it so decided. ... To be deprived of my liberty at the hands of my family or friends or

fellow citizens is to be deprived of it just as effectively." (Berlin 1969/2002, p. 209)

If we wish to preserve our liberty, it is not enough to say it must not be violated unless someone authorizes it.

Civic Virtue: Skinner and Machiavelli

Skinner began the essay "The Idea of Negative Liberty: Machiavellian and Modern Perspectives" (1984/2002) with a summary of his view on the value of studying history. A purely analytical link between negative liberty with virtue and service would be dismissed out of hand as a confusion or a different concept all together. It would be unconvincing since it is intuitively obvious they can't be linked. Skinner however uses history to question rather than underpin our current beliefs. Machiavelli's argument about negative liberty has been forgotten but can be used to question the terms of current debate. Skinner shows that a different understanding of negative freedom was actually used rather than just his imagination. To write a usable philosophy of history it has been suggested that we concentrate on those passages where familiar concepts are used to construct familiar arguments with which we can debate. If a text is not a live issue for us, it is a part of the 'history of ideas' not philosophy. Therefore, it follows that if we can use a text to mirror back to us our own beliefs and assumptions it is philosophical, if not it is historical. The only way to learn from the past is to assimilate it, to find better answers to perennial problems. The relevance of those parts of the past that we don't recognize as immediately applicable, may be that they enable us to stand back from our beliefs and concepts to rethink them.

Hobbes said liberty was simply the absence of opposition, nothing else. He opposed the idea that liberty can only be guaranteed in a particular form of self-government, that personal freedom depends on performing public service, and the qualities needed to ensure the effective performance of such duties are the civic virtues. Hobbes said liberty was freedom from public service. Isaiah Berlin said equating duty with interest would be either self-deceit or hypocrisy. The absence of constraint is unconnected with the pursuit of any determinate ends or substantive purposes. Individual liberty may be connected to virtue and public service if, as Aristotle held, we had an objective notion of *eudaimonia* or human flourishing, with certain true ends and rational purposes. If there is an essence to human nature its full realization may only be possible in a certain form of society. We may need to serve and uphold such a society if our true natures and individual liberty is to reach their fullest development. If we can find there are real and identifiably human interests, we may be able to suggest that only virtuous and public-spirited citizens have full possession of liberty. There must be some content to objective human flourishing if we are to link individual liberty, virtuous acts, and public service. "In an earlier and now discarded strand of thinking about social freedom, the concept of negative freedom was combined with the ideals of virtue and public service in just the manner nowadays assumed to be impossible without incoherence." (Skinner 2002, p. 190)

In *The Discourses* (1517/1970) Machiavelli clearly defines liberty as recognizably negative. It is to be unobstructed or unconstrained from acting according to one's own will and judgement. It is in our best interest to live in any type of community that would enable us to pursue our chosen ends. This could only be in a free society. Freedom for a government is the same as freedom for an individual; "to govern itself from the outset according to its own will, whether as a republic or a principality." I.2

While in theory a prince could rule in a way that reflects the general will, Machiavelli was skeptical. "It is not the pursuit of individual good, but of the common good, that makes cities great, and it is beyond doubt that it is only in republics that this ideal of the common good is properly served, because everything that promotes it is followed out." II.2 This is because princes and their court can be defensive about the prerogatives and policies they call their own; in a court each competes with the others for the prince's favour. If we wish to foster the common good and have our individual liberty consequently upheld, we must institute and maintain elective self-government. Negative liberty in today's debate denies any necessary connection between the maximizing of individual liberty and the upholding of any particular form of government, Machiavelli disagreed. We need a republic.

Machiavelli's theory of human nature was that there are two types of citizen, with different understandings of what it means to flourish. I.16 The *grandi* who sought to use their *virtu* to win power and glory. And the *plebe* or *popolo* wanted security and an undisturbed way of life "without having any anxiety that their property will be taken away from them." II.2 Similarly, some countries like to live peacefully, while others want to conquer and dominate. Dangerous ambition can come from without or from within.

The threat from without is international war, which can be unavoidable when others want to conquer us. It is necessary for the prince to study the strategies of war, and to establish military ordinances that make all citizens defenders of their own liberty. It is effeminate and lazy to hire mercenaries. They will never fight to the death for the little pay they are given, while a citizen army will fight to the death to defend their homes. There are two virtues needed to be cultivated prudence and courage. The careful calculation of chances and outcomes should determine when to go to war, how to wage a campaign, and how to react and withstand changing fortunes. II.12 II.14 II.27 Courage or sheer determination can make the difference between victory or not. Fury is not enough; it must be disciplined by persistence into courage.

The danger of ambition coming from within the society is that the *grandi* may try to achieve power at the expense of fellow-citizens. They gather round themselves partisans, so they can take control of the government from the public. III.22 They do this through using their high social standing to overawe fellow-citizens to persuade them to adopt sectional interests over the good of the community. Or, they get re-elected so often they become sources of increasing patronage and personal loyalty. Then, they can use their wealth to buy support at the expense of the public interest. "From partisans arise factions in cities, and from factions their ruin." I.7

The first line of defence against dangerous ambition coming from inside the city is to have the right laws and ordinances. This should prevent anyone from exercising undue or coercive influence. Laws should express the general will, not the most active ambitious members. Government offices should be open to all citizens so that public institutions could curb selfish greed, ambition and factiousness. Unless this is done the intemperance of the *grandi* will lead to tyranny. The virtues needed are prudence and temperance/orderliness. No community is well ordered unless by a wise and prudent ruler, that was how Rome maintained her liberty so long. Civic affairs must be debated and decided in an orderly and well-tempered style; "to give their opinion without passion, and then modestly and without passion to defend it." III.35 We have a duty to advise the public. As long as intemperate and disorderly conduct is permitted the result will be tyranny. If the virtues of prudence and temperance are practiced freedom can be preserved for a long time. I.7

To recap, Machiavelli's understanding was that in order to be free we need a free society, we need to serve this society, and the best way to do that is the civic virtues, all while maintaining a negative conception of liberty. A readiness to patriotically volunteer for active military service is necessary for maintaining liberty from being conquered and enslaved. The virtues needed are prudence and courage. The only way to prevent the *grandi* from coercing the *popolo* into serving their ends is to make sure every citizen has a chance to play a part in public office, volunteering for public service. Doing good for the community is a way of maintaining liberty and avoiding tyranny and dependence. The virtues needed are prudence and temperance. The *virtu* needed to secure liberty are courage, temperance/orderliness, and prudence. All cardinal virtues. This is a purely classical formulation to be found in Machiavelli. What makes him different is that he does not include justice. In both war and peace injury is sometimes indispensable. We need a certain ruthlessness to discount justice when necessary for the common good.

In the debate today what philosophers take to be general truths about concepts are really only true of their own theories. It is thought that negative liberty is all about rights. Machiavelli didn't mention rights. He thought negative liberty was not about securing rights but the performance of social duties. However, the reason for cultivating virtue and serving the common good is not that they are our duties, but that they form the best defence of our liberty. This is clear and not very metaphysical. Unless evil men can be given selfish reasons to act virtuously they won't do so. Skinner proved that in Machiavelli negative liberty is compatible with a theory of human nature that needs a particular type of polity, a republic, and that the best way to serve this is the virtues.

Laws

There should be some freedom to make our choices morally praiseworthy. Laws however are necessary so people are not tempted to use force or fraud. According to Machiavelli the laws can take self-centered individuals and force them to protect their freedom as in a citizen's army. Other self-destructive and antisocial behaviour can be curbed by having penalties attached to them. The law can coerce us to respect our freedom and that of others. This is definitely not positive freedom where a lower-self is aligned with a higher-self, the selfish part is kept and used to obtain compliance out of a fear of penalty. In any case, liberty is defined negatively by Skinner/Machiavelli as the absence of interference, though Skinner still wants to keep Rousseau's paradoxical adage 'forced to be free' and thinks Machiavelli shows how. Philip Pettit sees a more positive higher calling for the law in a constitution that can embed the rule of law, separation of powers, and protection against the majority. All of which are designed to thwart the arbitrary will of governors. The laws may interfere but they don't have to impose any arbitrary domination of their own, so long as they serve the interests of the people according to their ideas and there are avenues to redress this. Similar to the virtue of citizenship, we need to be able to own and identify with the process and decisions made, especially if we don't get our way.

Skinner and Machiavelli

In "Machiavelli on *Virtu* and the Maintenance of Liberty" (1983/2002) Skinner went against prevailing assumptions about negative liberty. The Modern side sees laws only as limitations to our freedoms, justified by protecting the freedom of others. While the Classical side saw that good laws can force us to maintain our freedom.

There are two rival views as to why it is difficult to maintain our freedom. John Rawls sees the danger arises from our selfishness. We all want to promote our freedom to the greatest extent possible, even to the detriment of others. We must limit our liberty so we don't interfere with the liberty of others. Machiavelli thought freedom depended on a free society, based on free institutions in which all citizens participate, not subject to the will of particular individuals or groups, conquerors or tyrants. It is only when everyone puts their talents at the disposal of the common good or public interest that factional conflicts can be overcome. *Virtu* was the willingness "to follow to the uttermost whatever course of action will in fact save the life and preserve the liberty of one's native land." III.41

We could be mistaken about what is in our best interest. There can be genuine objective reasons for action unconnected with current desires. Most citizens are corrupt and would put their private interests before the common good. Ordinary people are *ozioso,* too lazy to devote themselves to civic obligations. Even more dangerous however is *ambizione*, where prominent citizens want to pervert free institutions to promote their own family or group. The problem is not selfishness, but that in pursuing our self-interest we can be deceived about the best means of attaining our goals, including maintaining our liberty. If we are *ozioso* we may think freedom is to be left alone to do our own thing without demands on our time. *Ambizione* thinks freedom is getting what we want, using institutions for our own ends. When we allow policies hostile to the common good we undermine the free institutions that protect our liberty.

"The people, deceived by a false image of the good, very often will their own ruin." I.53

The reason we are blind to our best interest is that politicians lie about the right course of action to further their desired ends; they would propose laws that serve their own power not public liberty. They might dazzle us with their greatness and authority, using their gifts to seize power for themselves. Or, they may use their wealth to purchase loyalty and raise private armies to threaten the republic. People may not see their freedom is being threatened because they have been bribed to look the other way. Corrupted by bribes, the young may prefer licence for themselves rather than liberty for all. This way they destroy the freedom of the city and its citizens. Corruption must be stopped if we are to avoid self-destructive and anti-social behaviour.

Machiavelli places all his faith in the coercive power of the law to protect liberty. The fear of punishment makes the law effective and can help keep *ambizione* down. It deters us from *corruzione* or corruption and leads us to behaving *virtuousi* by making it less tempting to follow our interests at the expense of the common good. The law can coerce us in such a way as to promote the public interest even while pursuing our own selfish interests. This is not the same as bringing our desires in line with a higher self. Since we still keep our selfish patterns with their self-destructive tendencies.

What kind of laws did Machiavelli have in mind? A constitution is a good start. "No republic can ever hope to become perfect unless she provides for everything by means of her laws and furnishes a remedy for dealing with every possible accident." I.34 "always recognizing the necessity of creating new *ordini* when new necessities arose in the handling of their city's affairs." I.49 To protect the city from foreign invasion Machiavelli suggested raising a citizen army in advance, so the people could defend themselves. There should be a *Guardia della liberta*, a special magistracy dedicated to protecting the freedom of a citizen from another citizen's interference. There should be set terms to public offices for limited periods so that a civil or military authority does not grow to assume power away from the community; against bribery Machiavelli thought it was best to keep the public rich and the private poor. Both Rawls and Machiavelli agree to a bicameral legislature. For Machiavelli the Roman Senate had two groups representing the opposing interests of the elites and the *plebes,* with each maintaining a watch over the other so that purely sectional proposals were blocked. This internal conflict kept Rome's freedom for a long time, with each side voting against the unjust laws of the other. For Rawls religion is a danger since intolerant believers may want to convert or persecute others. While for Machiavelli, Christianity had said our salvation was more important than love of one's country, that was disloyal and corrupt. He wanted *ordini* to promote religion so people's superstitions could be manipulated for the common good, such as swearing and keeping one's oaths or having to face God's wrath.

For someone like Rawls we must fairly adjudicate competing rational egoists so that we don't threaten the freedom of others. But for Machiavelli the issue is transforming self-destructive *corruzione* or corruption into a *virtuouso* concern for the common good. There must be a way to prevent our inescapable *ozio* or *amizione* from having their natural but damaging effects. For Rawls the constitution is the best access to power, where we can prevent any infringement of our rights as well as offering the best capacity to defend our liberty. For Machiavelli the constitution converts private vices into public benefits, coercing us to respect our own freedom as well as other's. According to Berlin the law should create a neutral framework within which as many individuals as possible may achieve as many of their ends as possible without assessing their value, insofar as the freedom of others is respected. According to Machiavelli the law is also a liberating agent. If the law-makers are wise, laws will release us from bondage to our natural destructive selfishness, so that we are granted our freedom by being coerced.

Skinner is not as concerned in this essay to make precisely clear that Machiavelli's concept of freedom is a negative one, but he does show Machiavelli's theory of the law was not positive liberty. Skinner shows the laws can correct our motivations when we are wrong about our best interest, such as how to maintain our liberty. It does this for Machiavelli not by trying to align the lower-self with the higher-self, but by accepting the selfish nature of man which it disciplines. Thus it was not positive liberty. The law is not all restraint, however, but does have a further liberating effect. The law can force us to respect our own and other's freedom. Philip Pettit argues that while the law may interfere with our freedom, it does not have to arbitrarily dominate us. One liberating effect of the law is that it can stop others from arbitrarily interfering with us.

Philip Pettit

Modern History of "Liberty"

Philip Pettit does not accept Skinner's negative theory of liberty. He says there is a third possibility apart from negative and positive liberty. There is the absence of mastery by others, or non-domination. Like negative liberty it is marked by an absence. Unlike positive liberty freedom from the mastery of others does not guarantee self-mastery.

We can suffer domination without interference; such as a slave whose master is generous and lets the slave do whatever he wants. We can also suffer interference without domination; "the interference promises to further my interests, and promises to do so according to opinions of a kind I share." (Pettit 1997, p.23) Here interference is not arbitrary. The slave does not enjoy their freedom with any degree of security, if conditions change an interference on an arbitrary basis follows.

Under non-domination no one has that arbitrary power over you. Non-domination is a robust ideal of liberty. It is necessary for someone to be free that they are not subject to someone else's mastery. It is sufficient because when the law tracks one's interests and ideas there is still some sense in which they are free. The republican ideal was not positive freedom either; liberty is freedom from arbitrary interference, democratic self-rule either participatory or representative is merely a means to the end of furthering liberty. It was only Rousseau who had later said republican liberty was populist democracy.

In the republican tradition the contrast between a citizen and a slave goes as far back as Rome. Machiavelli said subjection to tyranny and colonization were forms of slavery. Just after the English Civil War (1642–1651), in 1656 James Harrington said "the man that cannot live on his own must be a servant, but he that can upon his own may be a freeman." (as quoted in Pettit 1997, p.32) Freedom demands material resources. Unfreedom is to live at the arbitrary will of another as a slave. The vulnerability of depending on the grace and favour of another is the absence of freedom. Harrington inspired the commonwealth movement. In the 1680's Algernon Sydney wrote "liberty solely consists in an independency upon the will of another." (as quoted in Pettit 1997, p.33) and just because the master allows the slave to do what they want he is still "a slave who serves the best and gentlest man in the world." *Cato's Letters* said "Liberty is to live upon one's own terms; Slavery is to live at the mere Mercy of another." (Pettit 1997, p. 33) In the early eighteenth century the commonwealthmen celebrated emancipation from the Stuart absolutism in terms of freedom from slavery. The American colonies complained about taxation without representation. Richard Price argued they were not free citizens but subject to arbitrary control. The colonists felt they had no control over Britain which was an ocean away, so they were slaves subject to the arbitrary will of parliament.

The non-domination of non-arbitrary law was also a tradition in the republican thought inspired by Harrington. They believed that it was possible for liberty to be lost without actual interference, and interference can occur without any loss of liberty. Moderns would say that the restriction of law is compensated for by preventing even more interference. But republicans held that citizenship was only possible under the rule of law, as long as they are not under any one individual's or group's arbitrary will. Good laws protect us from the arbitrary will of another, hopefully without introducing any new dominating force themselves. Law is not arbitrary when interference is in the pursuit of the common interests of citizens in a manner that conforms to their opinions. Without the right sort of law there is no liberty. There is freedom when laws are written by individuals for the protection of individuals. For Machiavelli, if the law-makers are wise, laws will release us from bondage to our natural selfishness, the constitution converts private vices into public benefits, coercing us to respect our own freedom as well as other's.

The idea that the law creates liberty was mocked by Hobbes in the seventeenth century just as the English civil war was underway. He said it made no difference whether we were ruled by a republic or an absolute monarch because freedom was the same for both, the absence of interference, physical coercion or threat. The law is always an invasion of liberty. It is only the silence of the laws that allows for freedom. There may be more laws in a republic. Hobbes' definition of liberty was used by John Lind in opposition to Richard Price, and was rehearsed by the Tory opponents to the American Revolution. The colonies were not slaves but in the same position of freedom as England, restricted by law. Civil liberty was not the same as natural liberty in the state of nature. The law restrains natural liberty, which was according to the republicans not really liberty but licence. Identifying 'liberty' with natural liberty helped sideline the republican talk of civil liberty. After the English Civil War and the American Revolution Harrington seemed to have won the debate with Hobbes.

Jeremy Bentham thought he invented Hobbes' definition of negative freedom. This only showed that Hobbes had been put on the shelf of historical curiosities to be forgotten, until the argument was needed to dismiss the complaints of servitude and domination coming from the American colonists. Bentham became more reformist and progressive as he came to influence English political thought. He came to see the American Revolution more favourably, but he kept the definition of liberty as the absence of coercion and is the one who did the most to establish it in modern thought.

Also important was William Paley another utilitarian thinker. He said those who see liberty as security against arbitrary interference are confusing means and ends. Non-interference was more scientific and could come in degrees rather than being black or white. The republican ideal was too demanding and did not represent a sensible goal. It is unobtainable in experience inflaming expectations that could never be satisfied and disturbs the public with complaints about which nothing can be done.

Liberalism came next, which has remained current past Isaiah Berlin and John Rawls. Under the ancient republic offices could only be open to property-holding mainstream males. It has seemed politically incorrect to call employees and women slaves, however. Non-domination came to seem impossible when it was common prejudice that their positions will always remain subordinate. Liberals saw that as we increased more and more people as citizens, it was unrealistic to remain with the old ideal that had only applied to independent rich males. Liberals who see themselves as progressive have come to accept Hobbes' absolutist definition of negative liberty.

Definition of Domination

Pettit defines domination as the capacity for an intentional negative influence on what another chooses:

1. They have the capacity to interfere
2. On an arbitrary basis
3. In certain choices that the other is in a position to make.

Interference is not a bribe or reward. It makes things worse for the dominated. It is intentional negligence not an accident. It can be coercion of the body as in restraint, or the will as in punishment or the threat there of, and it can be back-doors manipulation of the range of options, the expected payoffs, or the actual payoffs. The removal of an option is either/or but the expected or actual costs are greater or smaller. Context is important, such as an omission, or exploiting someone's urgent needs to drive a hard bargain. It need not always involve a wrongful act. It is does not necessarily need any actual interference as in the slave, but a capacity ready to be exercised, though not a virtual one yet to be developed.

Arbitrariness is when the dominating agent can choose to interfere at their pleasure, their judgement and will. They are not forced to follow the interests of the dominated according to their ideas. Domination is unchecked. In the case of taxes or punishment the relevant interests and ideas will be shared in common, we cannot make an exception for ourselves. Non-domination does not seek the dominators welfare and worldview, but those of the public where people can speak for themselves or for their groups. Every interest and idea should be open to challenge from anywhere in society, and when there is dissent we should find appropriate remedies. Arbitrariness can be more or less intense. Parliamentary procedures and certain legal conditions can help screen and filter out unsuitable acts. Penalties for violence and fraud, or making public officials accountable for their ulterior motives, can expose arbitrary interference to sanction.

Our choices must be ones that we are capable of making, not mere incapacities. The definition includes only "certain choices," someone can dominate some areas of our choices but not all. It can vary in extent and intensity; domination should be limited to fewer areas with less importance. The extent of the compromise of our liberty is what undermines us. Non-domination is compromised by domination alone. We can extend non-domination by stopping people from being able to arbitrarily interfere. The intensity is of the conditions that determine the incapacity to do something, such as natural, cultural, or legal limitations. We can increase the intensity by reducing conditioning factors and increasing the range and ease of non-dominated choices.

There is a mutual common knowledge about domination between those with or without arbitrary power.

The powerless are not going to be able to look the powerful in the eye, conscious as each will be – and conscious as each will be of the other's consciousness – of this asymmetry. Both will share an awareness that the powerless can do nothing except by the leave of the powerful: that the powerless are at the mercy of the powerful and not on equal terms. (Pettit 1997, p. 60-1)

The powerful feel they can control, the dominated feel vulnerable. There is fear and deference, not frankness. Except when there is manipulation, which is usually covert. Non-domination is also common knowledge, with the ability to look the other in the eyes. I know that you know that I know you know you can't control me, by right. This affects our self-image.

The liberal tradition in Pettit's eyes hold that freedom can be contrasted with the feeling of freedom, and hence without common subjective or intersubjective recognition and awareness. Non-interference can be enjoyed alone without special devices, but non-domination needs protective institutions to ensure this and testify to it. If we are against domination but not interference as such, we will be more accepting of state interference when it is not arbitrary but serves our interests according to our ideas.

Non-interference can be practiced alone, but non-domination is in the midst of others, where no one has the ability to dominate another. It is either/or. One should be able to pursue choices as an officially recognized right. This cannot be done for one unless it is done for all. There should be no fear and deference at another's grace and mercy. Authorities should lose any power of arbitrary control. Non-domination pays attention to three qualities of slavery non-interference can ignore: insecurity, deference, and social subordination.

Consent to interference, however, is not sufficient to eliminate arbitrariness. Rousseau came up with the populist idea that consent meant the majority rules, which can dominate a minority. The idea of a 'free contract' where, since we can choose to enter or not and negotiate its terms, this legitimizes any treatment one party accepts from the other. We don't need consent so much as the permanent possibility of contesting power. We need contest the abuse a government does, not form some popular will.

What should we do to redress arbitrary interference? Reciprocal power is one that tries to make the level between the less and more powerful more equal, so they can better defend themselves. This usually means punishing the interference, but this creates its own domination and interference. A constitutional authority, on the other hand, will not dominate if their interference is in the interests of the people according to their ideas, the common good. The only way to test this is to have public hearings to make it possible to voice complaints and contest the interference of authorities. We learn, and promote the common good, by having our policies contested and appropriate amendments made.

Constitutional Safeguards

We minimize the arbitrariness of the state through a constitution. A good constitution is one that can't be manipulated. A love of the constitution goes back to Rome, but the fear of being 'manipulated' is a more recent development. There are three conditions that serve to thwart the will of those in power, making government more difficult to arbitrarily organize. These constitutional suggestions have run throughout the republican tradition.

1. Rule of law. Laws must obey the standards accepted in jurisprudence today. Those who can make laws without being subject to them, make retrospective laws that only apply to particular people, or unpromulgated laws that are obscure and inconsistent, all have arbitrary power. Where there is a choice between acting on a legal basis or in a more particular way case by case, government officials should prefer a principled approach.

2. Dispersion of power. This includes the division of powers, a bicameral legislature, a federal system, and the United Nations. Functions should be split among different people to avoid absolute arbitrary power. Putting more than one power or function in anyone's hand would enable them to play with the law unregulated. If legislators are to write legislation in a way to be consistent with existing laws, those who judge whether it does so conform should not be the legislators themselves. It is important that those who execute the laws are not their own judges.

   There is no need for water-tight regimentation, the *Federalist Papers* thought some overlap would keep each branch watching the others, jealously protecting their jurisdictions. But for the populist any bleeding of jurisdictions would give more power to the executive or judiciary than the people and their representatives. They want a strict separation of powers.

3. Counter-majoritarian conditions. The more basic and important laws must not be subject to straightforward majoritarian amendment. It should not be easy to change the more basic and important laws, such as a constitution which constrains the more common laws that people *may* change. It should take more than a parliamentary or popular majority. Constitutional amendments should have to pass a difficult process; such as being passed by two houses, a majority of electors in a majority of states, or a two-thirds majority. There must also be an entrenched bill of rights to protect minorities.

Democracy

Contestability is necessary because we cannot hope to have a law for every occasion, there must be some discretion for those who legislate, execute, or judge the law. What is important is if private or factional inclinations and opinions rule then the people are at the mercy of authorities and must "bow and scrape" to appease them. (Pettit 1997, p. 184) Decision-making should not be the impositions of the will of a master, but one with which we can own and identify, where our interests are furthered and our ideas respected. It must accord with our ways of caring and thinking.

A traditional line is that one would own a decision if one consented to it, but if we had to obtain every individual's consent it would be impossible. If we allowed for implicit consent, then it would be so accessible as to be meaningless. Collective consent is no better, majority support can arbitrarily interfere with the lives of minorities. Democracy as consent can be seen in the popular elections of the members of the legislature, which may be inappropriate for those areas that need expertise such as executive committees or the judiciary. These must still be democratically accountable.

What matters is not the history of origins in consent, but the modal counterfactual of passing possible contestation. Pettit defines democracy as "the extent that the people individually and collectively enjoy a permanent possibility of contesting what government decides." (Pettit 1997, p. 185) People are capable of testing their beliefs and desires especially when problems arise and whether they retain their commitments depend on how well they survive our tests. A self-ruling individual may run on automatic pilot most of the time, on beliefs and desires with long forgotten origins, but they are not just the victims of their beliefs and desires they may examine these at will and maintain or amend them. For a self-ruling demos decision-making may materialize under unexamined routines as in common law, but we do not have to accept any pattern of decision-making that arises, we can protest there is a mismatch with the relevant interests and opinions forcing an amendment. Contestation does not necessarily involve the consensus of majority decision-making. Democracy simply provides an environment for the selection of laws. To the extent that laws survive critical scrutiny they can be presumed to answer the interests and ideas of the people. If government is a form of legal trust, then people can challenge how far and how well it is discharging that trust. The sovereignty of the people does not lie in electoral authorization but in the right to resist.

Pettit compares contestatory democracy with interest-group pluralism. Contestatory democracy foregrounds reason in that public decisions must be transparently based on neutral considerations. Interest-group pluralism backgrounds reason since they think the best way to organize public life is to have a framework so things will happen according to reason, defined as

175

preference satisfaction, even if each only looks out for themselves. The invisible hand of the free-market is an example they would apply to politics, where citizens vote for the party that promises to satisfy their personal interests the best, while legislators vote for policies that will get them re-elected. According Mandeville private vices lead to public benefits. The way to get the best public results was thought not to have citizens internalize the common good and deliberate how to promote it, but to have everyone look after themselves and rely on the framework to ensure that everything will lead to the maximization of the good. Interest-based pluralism makes self-seeking the motor of political life, which can subject the weak to the naked preferences of the strong who have more resources. Republicans do not have to be against the free-market, however. If there are no great differences of bargaining power, a free-market does not have to expose us to domination.

A decision is democratic when those who make it are accountable to the ordinary people they affect. There are three preconditions for contestability:

1. The basis of the republic must be deliberative.

    This is not the bargaining of interest groups, which begins with pre-given desires and trades concessions to reach a mutually beneficial agreement, with each looking to offer the least concessions from themselves. The bargain paradigm would contest a decision if it did not stick to the original contract and demanded a concession the other is unwilling to make. Bargaining is only possible if one has enough negotiating power to threaten the other's compliance, as an interest group that pulls some weight.

    In debating we interrogate each other about the nature and importance of our considerations, converging on an answer as to what arrangement best answers the considerations everyone recognizes as relevant. There should be enough common ground for conversation, but short of complete agreement there must be room for challenging arguments recognized as relevant by all sides. In debating we can protest unsuitable reasons that do not answer very well all the relevant considerations. Debate is open to anyone who can plausibly challenge a reasoned decision, it does not theoretically depend on having clout. Preferences are formed by debate, not given.

Officials must make clear what motivates them. There must be procedures for identifying relevant considerations, enabling citizens to question whether these are the relevant ones. And, there must be a procedure to tell whether these have in fact determined the outcome.

2. The voice of the republic must be inclusive. People have a voice insofar as they can speak out and affect the proposed legislation.

There must be room to protest representative bodies when things have not been done properly. There should a way to complain and appeal, to state a grievance and demand satisfaction, well established in the community. This can include a letter to your member of Parliament, an inquiry by an ombudsman, or appealing to a higher court, as well as activities involving our rights of association, protest, and demonstration. Social movements are most effective, they screen out complaints and those they do take up they can do with more noise than an individual.

Proportional representation is needed according to Pettit. Elections may serve to make legislators responsive to their constituents, but this may be inappropriate for the executive and judicial branches where expertise is more important than popularity. Experts must incorporate all the voices of difference found in a community so they can hear the full range of perspectives. Ideally a group will be represented, not by the grace of a senator, but by their own members. A certain minimum statistical representation of the population is required to ensure all sectors are listened to and all possibly relevant factors considered. It is important that government is not statistically dominated by any one religion, gender, class, or ethnicity. If they are unrepresentative, there is no guarantee other groups can make their voices heard.

The government will have to guard against powerful private interests. The rich who fund politicians have more of a say than the rest of us. We can limit private campaign contributions making them public, we can publicly fund candidates according to their merits or support, we may direct a limited portion of our tax or state allowance to the party of our choice, and we may ban or limit advertising.

3. The forum of the republic must be responsive, where people can receive a proper hearing.

A proper hearing can change our priorities. The common image of getting a hearing for some challenge involves a popular movement creating widespread controversy and debate followed by progressive legislative adjustment. It should be possible for people to coalesce around group identities that were once suppressed, or espouse various causes that were not salient, so they have the opportunity to bring others to their point of view. All this involves changing and evolving what we consider to be our interests. We need to give a hearing to evolving allegiances and commitments, open to deep and wide-ranging transformations.

There are two reasons a contestation may be denied. One is that the common interest may have to frustrate one party. The other is that it represents a minority judgement on the common interest. If this is not particularly important, those disappointed may recognize that people rationally differ, approve the decision process, and see it is a genuine attempt to determine the common interest.

Where the issue is of personal or cultural importance, in the worst case the disappointed cannot view the judgement as anything but arbitrary; it was not a decision dictated by an interest they share or made by a procedure they accept. Apart from secession, there should be room for conscientious objections where dissenting individuals or groups can claim special treatment under the law.

Again, the democratic basis for the republic must first be deliberative where we can collaborate on shaping the agenda, not the bargaining of interest groups with predetermined objectives. Secondly, the voice of the republic must be inclusive, where people can speak out and affect proposed legislation. There must be avenues of protest, proportional representation, and safeguards against powerful private interests. Thirdly, the forum of the republic must be responsive, where people can receive a proper hearing to affect what we see as our needs.

Conclusion and John Maynor

We can have good laws that not only make the antisocial self-destructive respect their own and other's freedom, but such things as a constitution can stop those who make or enforce the law from arbitrarily interfering with a citizen's choices. Skinner argued the republican did not have to believe in positive liberty, Machiavelli didn't. Pettit said that it was Rousseau who later put the populist element into self-government, which was revived by

Hannah Arendt's ideal of participatory democracy. According to Skinner Machiavelli held to negative liberty, the freedom from interference. According to Pettit, the interference of wise laws does not have to create its own arbitrary domination. The law does not necessarily make us unfree if it is stopping arbitrary domination and at the same time conforms to our values and opinions of fairness and justice. Pettit said that as long as there are avenues for redressing grievances we can feel comfortable that the legislation that survives the long run serves our interests and standards.

Pettit said the history of the origin of legislation in consensus was not what's important, but the modal counter-factual of being able to pass possible contestation. Alasdair MacIntyre (1988) said a tradition can always go through an epistemic crisis in which it may be retained, modified, or discarded. This is forever a possibility as long as the tradition is alive. This is a modal possibility, the necessary possibility of an open question.

G. E. Moore said for any time someone said the Good = X, it makes sense to ask but is X good? Meaning the good is a non-natural property of which we are intuitively aware, neither a tautology nor an empirical fact. But we don't have to accept the idea of another world, we can accept there is a non-natural element of infinity in any normative statement. We could always be wrong and not know it until it was brought to our attention somehow. This is forever an open possibility, a necessary possibility. That is why the ability to contest public decisions is so important. We should always be willing to test ourselves and improve. Perfection is infinite, we can always learn.

Even if the whole decision-making process does not involve any domination we may still come up with a law that does. Pettit wants avenues to be open for contesting the decisions of government, such as writing a letter to one's member of Parliament, getting an inquiry by an ombudsman, or appealing to a higher court. Or, activities involving our rights of association, protest, and demonstration. However, there are more ways of getting involved in civic affairs than just protesting. There have to be ways for hearings to include all the opinions and values of those who will be affected by a policy, before it is implemented. If a group is not heard faithfully from the beginning it may take more and more concessions down the road to reconcile with them later on. Does this have to imply consensus? No, as long as we can own and identify with the process and decisions being made as fair, we can understand when we don't get our way. One way to identify with the decision-making process is to volunteer on government committees. A good society would be one that allows for open avenues of civic participation and expression in a way that can make a difference.

It has been argued that it is better to work for consensus, where we may not end up with our first choice but everyone can agree to it, rather than to vote and create exclusion with well-entrenched political oppositions. Pettit does not want to be like Rousseau where the consensus of majority rule can run roughshod over the rights of minorities. He does not want to espouse positive liberty as portrayed by Berlin. Therefore, he promotes routes for contestation. This can actually help perfect our government, as we come closer to minimizing domination. But the government must be proactive in searching out the opinions and interests of the populace, and the population must participate enough to articulate what these are, even if its just voting or answering polls and questionnaires. The citizen needs to be educated through deliberation with others about what our common goods are and how we can serve them through which civic virtues.

In civil society, one can donate time and money to an environmental cause or a social movement, which can raise more attention to the voices of those who share those values. There is a question, however, as to what kind of values a civic group promotes. According to Simone Chambers and Jeffrey Kopstein (2006) liberal democracy depends on reproducing democratic virtues such as tolerance, cooperation, and respect. In good civil society, people see those with whom they deeply disagree as deserving respect. Bad civil society promotes hatred and bigotry. Chambers and Kopstein asked whether we should only support those groups who promote civility, or will that undermine associational freedom?

According to John Maynor (2003) just as it is the case that I should not be dominated, so it is that I should not dominate. This is a valuable and definitively progressive advancement on Pettit's argument, further refining it. To do this it is first of all necessary to discover what other's interests are and respond appropriately. We must consider how our actions will affect others, treating them with civility and mutual respect in a way that does not provoke reproach. This takes the virtues of listening and articulating responses, as well as the willingness to accept decisions that go against one's preferences. Having to spell out my interests to others can lead to a deeper and richer understanding of what these are and listening should help us understand the perspective of others.

Maynor argued the state must actively endorse citizenship and civic virtue. If the state is to promote nondomination it cannot remain neutral to ideas of the good life. It has to support those lifestyles that are nondominating and make accountable those that are not. The state also needs to develop a certain kind of character in its citizens, where they identify their good with the traditions of the community in a nondominating manner. People who only look out for their own narrow private interests are more likely to use, dominate, manipulate, or arbitrarily interfere with the choices of others, even if what they do may not be a crime.

Making people accountable and forcing them to answer for themselves will supposedly educate their self-interested desires so they identify their good with that of society. We cannot make an exception for ourselves. We must have the ability to critically reflect on our actions and how they may arbitrarily interfere with others and impact the rest of society. Taking other's interests seriously with respect we can use communication and accommodation to encourage civility and trust as we address and negotiate our common problems.

The reciprocal nature of nondomination gives our civic virtue a quality and direction, a function and purpose. The telos is to find and articulate our true aims and goals in a way that respectfully tracks those of other's. This constitutes nondomination. Tolerance and respect for those who are different from us is a part of the decorum and etiquette needed for civic activities, which can create even more meaningful options and choices for us to actualize ourselves. Working together for the same goals we should incorporate different perspectives. I would add that when we feel we belong as members to a group or tradition this can help motivate us when we are discouraged and the odds seem overwhelming. Then we won't feel so alone.

Bibliography

Arendt, H. (1958). *The Human Condition*. Chicago: U of C
Press.

Arendt, H. (1963). *On Revolution*. NY: Penguin Books.

Austin, J. (1962). *How to Do Things withWords*. Oxford:
Oxford Clarenden Press.

Berlin, I. (1969/2002). Two Concepts of Liberty. In I. Berlin,
Liberty (pp. 166-217). Oxford: Oxford UP.

Bevir, M. (2011). The Contextual Approach. In G. Klosko,
*The Oxford Handbook of the History of Political
Philosophy* (pp. 11-23). Oxford: Oxford UP.

Bosanquet, B. (1890). *The Philosophical Theory of the
State*. London: Macmillon and Co.

Boyd, R. (1988). How to be a Moral Realist. In G. Sayre-
McCord, & G. Sayre-McCord (Ed.), *Essays on Moral
Realism* (pp. 181-228). N.Y., N.Y.: Cornell UP.

Cambridge School

Chambers, Simone and Kopstein, Jeffrey. (2006). Civil
Society and the State. In J. S. Dryzeck, B. Honig, A.
Philips, & B. H. JohnS. Dryzek (Ed.), *The Oxford
Handbook of Political Theory* (pp. 363-381). N.Y.,
N.Y.: Oxford UP.

Dahl, R. (1956). *A Preface to Democratic Theory.* Chicago:
U of C Press.

Dunn, J. (1972). The Identity of the History of Ideas.
Philosophy, Politics and Society, 158-173.

Dunning, W. A. (1902). *A History of Political Theories:
Ancient and Medieval.* NY: Macmillan.

Dunning, W. A. (1905). *A History of Political Theories: from
Luther to Montesquieu.* NY: Macmillan.

Dunning, W. A. (1920). *A History of Political Theories: from
Rousseau to Spencer.* NY: Macmillan.

Easton, D. (1953). *The Political System.* NY: Alfred A. Knopf.

Farr, J. (2006). The History of Political Thought as

Disciplinary Genre. In J. S. Dryzeck, B. Honig, & A.

Philips, *The Oxford Handbook of Political Theory*

(pp. 225-241). Oxford: Oxford UP.

Fink, Z. S. (1945). *The Classical Republicans: An Essay on

the Recovery of a Pattern of Thought in

Seventeenth-Century.* Eugene: Resource

Publications.

Flanagan, C. A. (2004). Citizenship. In M. Seligman, & C.

Peterson, *Character Strengths and Virtues: A

Handbook and Classification* (pp. 369-389). Oxford:

Oxford UP.

Foucault, M. (1971/1984). Nietzsche, Genealogy, History.

In M. Foucault, *The Foucault Reader* (pp. 76-100).

NY: Vintage Books.

Foucault, M. (1972/1980). On Popular Justice: A Discussion

with Maoists. In M. Foucault, *Power/Knowledge:*

Selected Interviews and Other Writingsn1972-1977 (pp. 1-36). NY: Vintage Books.

Foucault, M. (1977/1984). Truth and Power. In M. Foucault, *The Foucault Reader* (pp. 51-75). NY: Vintage Books.

Foucault, M. C. (2006). *Chomsky vs. Foucault: A Debate on Human Nature.* New Press.

Gadamer, H. G. (1975). *Truth and Method.* (J. W. Marshall, Trans.) N.Y., N.Y.: Continuum.

Gunnell, J. G. (2013). Social Science and Ideology: The Case of Behaviouralism in American Political Science. In M. Freeden, L. T. Sargent, & M. Stears, *The Oxford Handbook of Political Ideologies* (pp. 73-89). Oxford: Oxford UP.

Hartz, L. (1955). *The Liberal Tradition in America: An Interpretation of American Political Thought since the Revolution.* NY: Harcourt, Brace.

Heidegger, M. (1926/1962). *Being and Time.* (J. M. Robinson, Trans.) N.Y., N.Y.: Harper Collins Pub.

Herring, P. (1929). *Group Representation before Congress.* Baltimore: John Hopkins Press.

Kaplan, Abraham and Lasswell, Harrold D. (1950). *Power and Society.* New Haven: Yale UP.

Kuhn, T. (1962). *The Structure of Scientific Revolutions.* Chicago: U of C Press.

Laski, H. (1917). *Studies in the Problem of Sovereignty.* New Haven: Yale UP.

Laski, H. (1919). *Authority in the Modern State.* New Haven: Yale UP.

Laslett, P. (1956). Introduction. *Philosophy, Politics and Society*, vii-xv.

Leiber, F. (1835). *Manual of Political Ethics.* Philadelphia: Lippencott.

Leiber, F. (1853). *Civil Liberty and Self-government.* Philadelphia: Lippencortt.

Levinas, E. (1961). *Totality and Infinity: An Essay on Exteriority.* Pittsburgh: Duquesne UP.

Levinas, E. (1974). *Otherwise than Being or Beyond Essence.* Pittsburgh: Duquesne UP.

Levinas, E. (1982). *Ethics and Infinity.* Pittseburgh: Duquesne UP.

Levinas, E. (1998). *Entre Nous: On Thinking of the Other.* NY: Columbia UP.

Levinas, E. (1999). *Alterity and Transcendence.* NY: Columbia UP.

Lippman, W. (1921). *Public Opinion.* NY: Harcourt, Brace.

Lippman, W. (1925). *The Phantom Public.* NY: Harcourt, Brace.

Lyotard, J.-F. (1979/1984). *The Postmodern Condition: A Report on Knowledge.* (G. B. Massumi, Trans.) Minneapolis, Minn.: University of Minnesota Press.

Machiavelli, N. (1517/1970). *The Discorses.* NY: Penguin Books.

MacIntyre, A. (1981). *After Virtue.* Notre Dame: University of Notre Dame Press.

MacIntyre, A. (1988). *Whose Justice? Which Rationality?* Notre Dame: U of ND Press.

Maynor, J. W. (2003). *Republicanism in the Modern World.* Malden: Blackwel Pub. Inc.

Merriam, C. E. (1925). *New Aspects of Politics.* Chicago: U of C Press.

Pettit, P. (1997). *Republicanism: A Theory of Freedom and Government.* Oxford: Oxford UP.

Pocock, J. A. (1972). Languages and their Implications: The Transformation of Political Thought. In J. G. Pocock, *Politics, Language, and Time* (pp. 3-41). Chicago : U of C Press.

Pocock, J. G. (1962/2009). The History of Political Thought: Amethodological Enquiry. In J. G. Pocock, *Political Thought and History: Essays on Theory and Method* (pp. 3-19). Cambridge: Cambridge UP.

Pocock, J. G. (1962/2009). The origins of study of the past: a comparative approach. In J. G. Pocock, *Political Thought and History: Essays and Theory and Method* (pp. 145-186). Cambridge: Cambridge UP.

Pocock, J. G. (1975). *The Machiavellian Moment: Florintine Political Thought and the Atlantic Republican Tradition.* Princeton: Princeton UP.

Pocock, J. G. (1985). Intoduction: State of the Art. In J. G. Pocock, *Virtue, Commerce, and History* (pp. 1-34). Cambridge: Cambridge UP.

Pocock, J. G. (1987/2009). Texts as events: reflections on the history of political thought. In J. G. Pocock, *Political Thought and History* (pp. 106-119). Cambridge: Cambridge UP.

Pocock, J. G. (1987/2009). The concept of a language and the metier d'historien: some considerations on practice. In J. G. Pocock, *Political Thought and History* (pp. 87-105). Cambridge: Cambridge UP.

Putnam, H. (1973/2000). Meaning and Reference. In E. D. Klemke, *Contemporary Analytic and Linguistic Philosphies* (pp. 418-427). NY: Prometheus Books.

Putnam, H. (2002). *The Collapse of the Fact/Value Dichotomy and Other Essays*. Cambridge: Harvard UP.

Putnam, R. (2000). *Bowling Alone: The Collapse and Revival of American Community*. N.J.: Princeton UP.

Raab, F. (1965). *The English Face of Machiavelli: A Changing Interpretation 1500-1700.* Toronto: U of T Press.

Rawls, J. (1971). *A Theory of Justice.* MA: Harvard UP.

Robbins, C. (1959). *The Eighteenth Century Commonwealthman.* NY: Atheneum.

Sabine, G. H. (1923). Pluralism: A Point of View. *American Political Science Review,* 17: 34-50.

Sabine, G. H. (1930). The Pragmatic Approach to Politics. *American Political Science Review,* 24: 865-885.

Sabine, G. H. (1939). *A History of Political Theory.* NY: Holt, Rinehart and Winston.

Sandel, M. (1982). *Liberalism and the Limits of Justice.* Cambridge: Cambridge UP.

Skinner, Q. (1969/2002). Meaning and Understanding in the History of Ideas. In Q. Skinner, *Visions of*

Politics Volume 1: Regarding Method (pp. 57-89). Cambridge: Cambridge UP.

Skinner, Q. (1972/2002). Motives, Intentions and Interpretation. In Q. Skinner, *Visions of Politics Volume 1: Regarding Method* (pp. 90-102). Cambridge: Cambridge UP.

Skinner, Q. (1972/2002). 'Social Meaning' and the Explanation of Social Action. In Q. Skinner, *Visions of Politics Volume 1: Regarding Method* (pp. 128-144). Cambridge: Cambridge UP.

Skinner, Q. (1974/2002). Moral Principles and social change. In Q. Skinner, *Visions of Politics Volume 1: Regarding Method* (pp. 145-157). Cambridge: Cambridge UP.

Skinner, Q. (1978). *The Foundations of Modern Political Thought Volumr 1: The Renaissance.* Cambridge: Cambridge UP.

Skinner, Q. (1983/2002). Machiavelli on virtu and the maintenance of liberty. In Q. Skinner, *Visions of Politics Volume 2: Renaissance Virtues* (pp. 160-185). Cambridge: Cambridge UP.

Skinner, Q. (1984/2002). The idea of negative liberty: Machiavellian and modern perspectives. In Q. Skinner, *Visions of Politics Volume 2: Renaissance Virtues* (pp. 186-212). Cambridge: Cambridge UP.

Truman, D. (1951). *The Governmental Process.* NY: Knopf.

Wolin, S. (1960/2004). *Politics and Vision.* NY: Princeton UP.